Unit 19: Into the

Unit Description:

God's plan to save people from ~~~~~~~~~~~~~~~ Jesus was born at last. When Jesus grew up, He began His mission to bring people back to God. From the beginning, Jesus proved that He is the Son of God and that all that was written about Him by the prophets was true.

Unit 20: Prepare the Way

Unit Description:

Jesus grew up and began to prepare for His ministry. When Jesus was baptized, God confirmed His sonship. Jesus was subsequently tempted by Satan, but He did not sin.

Unit 21: Among the People

Unit Description:

As Jesus traveled throughout Judea, His personal encounters with ordinary people changed their lives in extraordinary ways. Jesus revealed that He was God the Son in human form, living among God's people and bringing salvation in Him alone.

Unit 19 · Session 1
From Adam to Jesus

BIBLE PASSAGE:
Matthew 1; Luke 3; John 1

STORY POINT:
Jesus' family line proved
He is the Messiah.

KEY PASSAGE:
John 1:1-2

BIG PICTURE QUESTION:
Is Jesus God or a human?
As the Son of God, Jesus is both
fully God and fully human.

INTRODUCE THE STORY (10–15 MINUTES) PAGE 6	TEACH THE STORY (25–30 MINUTES) PAGE 8	APPLY THE STORY (25–30 MINUTES) PAGE 14

 → →

Additional resources are available at gospelproject.com. For free training and session-by-session help, visit ministrygrid.com/gospelproject.

LEADER Bible Study

The prophecies concerning Jesus' birth are numerous, and many of them refer to Jesus' lineage. Old Testament prophecies tell of the promised Messiah being born from the seed of a woman (Gen. 3:15); from the seed of Abraham (Gen. 22:18), Isaac (Gen. 21:12), and Jacob (Num. 24:17); from the tribe of Judah (Micah 5:2); from the line of Jesse (Isa. 11:1); and from the house of David (Jer. 23:5). The prophecies said He would be born of a virgin (Isa. 7:14) and would be the Son of God (1 Chron. 17:13-14; Ps. 2:7). Jesus fulfilled all of these prophecies.

In Bible times, Jews took great care to accurately record family genealogies. The family a person belonged to was directly linked to property rights. Matthew 1:1-17 and Luke 3:23-38 both chronicle the genealogy of Jesus. The account in Matthew presents Jesus as the king of the Jews—the legal heir to the throne of David. The account in Luke was written to Greek Christians and focuses on Jesus' descent from Adam.

Jesus was born as a baby in Bethlehem. He had earthly parents—Mary and Joseph—but His true Father is God. Jesus is fully God and fully man.

As fully God, "the entire fullness of God's nature dwells bodily in Christ" (Col. 2:9). As fully man, Jesus has a human body, human mind, and human emotions. (See Luke 2:7,52; Matt. 26:38.) He is our sinless representative (2 Cor. 5:21), sympathetic high priest (Heb. 4:15), and substitute sacrifice (1 John 4:10).

Use this Bible story with the kids you teach to review Jesus' ancestors and their stories in the Old Testament. Help kids recognize that God had been working out His plan to send Jesus over hundreds of years—through Adam, Abraham, Isaac, Rahab, Ruth, David, and others. God sent His Son to earth to save people from their sins.

The **BIBLE** Story

From Adam to Jesus
Matthew 1; Luke 3; John 1

Before He came to earth as a human being, **God the Son** was with the Father. No one created Him; He **has always existed.** God created the first people, Adam and Eve, but they did not obey Him. **All along, God planned to send His Son to earth to save people from sin. At just the right time, Jesus came to earth as a baby.** He was born to Mary, the wife of Joseph. **Jesus is different than any other baby who was ever born because He is fully God and fully human.**

Like all people on earth, Jesus' family had a history—a family tree. Jesus had parents, grandparents, great-grandparents, and great-great-grandparents … back and back for many generations. **Jesus was born into the family of Abraham and the family of King David. Abraham had a son named Isaac. When Isaac had a family, one of his sons was named Jacob. Jacob was part of Jesus' family. Years later, a man named Salmon** (SAL mahn) **was born into Jesus' family tree. He married Rahab** (RAY hab), who hid the Israelite spies when they came to Jericho. **Rahab had a baby named Boaz** (BOH az). **Boaz** was a farmer, and he **married Ruth. Boaz and Ruth had a son named**

Obed (OH bed).

Obed's son was Jesse. Jesse had many sons; his youngest was David. David was just a boy when he was chosen to be Israel's king. King David liked to write. He wrote songs—called psalms—and some of them were about the time when Jesus would come to earth.

Other people in Jesus' family were kings too. **David's son Solomon was a king. King Jehoshaphat** (jih HAHSH uh fat) **was part of Jesus' family, and so was Uzziah** (uh ZIGH uh), **Ahaz** (AY haz), **Hezekiah** (HEZ ih kigh uh), **and Josiah.**

God's people returned home from exile in Babylon. **Then Shealtiel** (shih AL tih el) **was born. His son was Zerubbabel** (zuh RUHB uh buhl). **Later, Matthan** (MAT than) **came along. Matthan's son was named Jacob, and Jacob's son was named Joseph. Joseph is the man who married Jesus' mother, Mary. Joseph raised Jesus as his own son. Jesus was truly God's Son—the Messiah.**

Christ Connection: Jesus came to earth as a human. Jesus had earthly parents, Mary and Joseph, but His true Father is God. Through Jesus, God kept His promises to Abraham and David. Jesus saves people from their sins and adopts them into God's family.

Bible Storytelling Tips

- **Display art:** Show art from previous Bible stories and point out people from the Bible story.
- **Show name tags:** Write names from the Bible story on index cards or adhesive labels. Display the names as you tell the story.

INTRODUCE the Story

SESSION TITLE: From Adam to Jesus
BIBLE PASSAGE: Matthew 1; Luke 3; John 1
STORY POINT: Jesus' family line proved He is the Messiah.
KEY PASSAGE: John 1:1-2
BIG PICTURE QUESTION: Is Jesus God or a human? As the Son of God, Jesus is both fully God and fully human.

Welcome time

Note: Be sensitive to kids' family situations.

Greet each kid as he or she arrives. Use this time to collect the offering, fill out attendance sheets, and help new kids connect to your group. Prompt kids to share about their families. Consider bringing photos of your family and telling kids the names of your family members.

Activity page (5 minutes)

· "Jesus Words" activity page, 1 per kid
· pencils or markers

Invite kids to complete "Jesus Words" on the activity page. Guide kids to make a list of words that describe Jesus. For an added challenge, prompt kids to list adjectives that begin with each letter of the alphabet. After a few minutes, invite volunteers to share their lists. If necessary, gently correct any misconceptions about Jesus.

SAY • Did anyone write down the word *human*? Jesus is God the Son, but did you know He came to earth and is both fully God and fully man? We will learn more about that today.

Session starter (10 minutes)

OPTION 1: Who's the one?

Instruct kids to stand up. Assign one kid to be *It*. *It* will stand in front of the players and decide which player is his *Person*. Then the players will take turns asking yes-or-no questions to determine who the *Person* is. (Examples: Is the *Person* a girl? Is the *Person* wearing black shoes? Does the *Person* have curly hair?)

If a player correctly identifies the *Person*, that player becomes *It* and chooses a new *Person* to begin a new round.

SAY • How many clues did you need before you figured out the chosen person? Long ago, God promised to send someone to rescue people from their sin. God said the Rescuer would come from the family of Abraham, Isaac, Jacob, Jesse, and David. Did Jesus fit that description? Today we will find out!

OPTION 2: Family faces

Form groups of three to six kids. Invite them to play a game similar to "Old Maid." Print four sets of the "Family Faces" cards for each group. Remove one card from each deck so each group has 27 cards (6 sets of 4 cards and 1 set of 3 cards). Mix up the cards and distribute them facedown. Players do not need to have an equal number of cards.

· "Family Faces" printable

Players will set aside any matches in their hands. To begin, a player takes one card from another player's hand. If that card completes a pair, the player sets aside the match. Then the next player selects a card from any other player. Continue until one card (from the set of three) remains.

SAY • Jesus' Father is God, but Jesus had a family on earth too. The Bible tells us about Jesus' ancestors: His parents, Mary and Joseph, all the way back to King David, Isaac, Abraham, Noah, and Adam.

Transition to teach the story

TEACH the Story

SESSION TITLE: From Adam to Jesus
BIBLE PASSAGE: Matthew 1; Luke 3; John 1
STORY POINT: Jesus' family line proved He is the Messiah.
KEY PASSAGE: John 1:1-2
BIG PICTURE QUESTION: Is Jesus God or a human? As the Son of God, Jesus is both fully God and fully human.

· room decorations
· Theme Background Slide (optional)

Suggested Theme Decorating Ideas: Simulate a portrait studio by hanging a large, solid-colored bedsheet or piece of paper against a wall. Position a chair or stool in front of the backdrop, and arrange two or three lights around the chair. Display portraits and other photography on a wall or on easels at one side. Consider including props, such as stuffed animals, costume jewelry, sports equipment, and so forth. You may also choose to project the theme background slide

Countdown

· countdown video

Show the countdown video as you transition to teach the story. Set it to end as the session begins.

Introduce the session (3 minutes)

· leader attire
· camera
· backpack
· family photo album
· Bible

Tip: If you prefer not to use themed content or characters, adapt or omit this introduction.

[Leader enters carrying a camera and a backpack. The backpack contains a family photo album and a Bible.]
LEADER • Hello, everyone! I'm *[your name]*, studio photographer. Raise your hand if you've ever had a photo portrait made. Maybe your family has had professional photos taken, or maybe your photo was taken at school. *[Pause for kids to respond.]* I enjoy taking photos for people to capture a moment in time. *[Show the photo album and Bible from your*

backpack.] Family portraits are my favorite. One time a big extended family—including cousins, aunts, uncles, and grandparents—came to my studio to get a photo together. I hope that family keeps the photo in a special place so their future children and grandchildren will treasure the photo many years from now. [*Hold up the Bible.*] Did you know the Bible tells us about Jesus' family? I can't wait for you to hear more.

Big picture question (1 minute)

LEADER • With today's Bible story and the stories we will hear in the coming weeks, we are going to answer a big picture question. Our big picture question helps us remember what God was doing all along. Our question today is about Jesus: *Is Jesus God or a human?* Now that's a great question. Jesus is God's Son, but He came to earth as a baby. Hmm, what do you think? *Is Jesus God or a human?* [*Allow kids to respond.*] Here's our answer: *As the Son of God, Jesus is both fully God and fully human.*

Giant timeline (1 minute)

Show the giant timeline. Point to individual Bible stories as you review.

• Giant Timeline

LEADER • The Bible stories we have heard so far have been from the Old Testament. The Old Testament tells us the history of the Jewish people. God created the world, and sin entered the world when Adam and Eve disobeyed God. God promised to bless the world through Abraham's offspring, and then God rescued the Israelites from slavery in Egypt. We learned about the Israelites' being ruled by judges and kings. Sometimes they obeyed God, and a lot of the time they disobeyed Him. God sent prophets to warn the people, but the people did not listen. God punished the people by sending them into exile. Then God brought His people back to their land.

All along, God had a plan to save His people from sin. He promised to send a Messiah. God planned for His Son, Jesus, to come to earth as a human, and today we will learn about Jesus' earthly family.

Tell the Bible story (10 minutes)

- Bibles
- "From Adam to Jesus" video
- Big Picture Question Poster
- Bible Story Picture Poster
- Story Point Poster

Open your Bible to Matthew 1; Luke 3; John 1. Use the Bible storytelling tips on the Bible story page to help you tell the story, or show the Bible story video "From Adam to Jesus."

LEADER • The Bible gives us so many names of people who were part of Jesus' family! **Jesus' family line proved He is the Messiah.** It stretches all the way back to Adam and Eve. Adam was the family representative for everyone born after him. The Bible calls Jesus "the last Adam." Death from sin came to the world through the first Adam; Jesus came to rescue sinners and bring life with God forever. [*See 1 Cor. 15:22,45.*]

Jesus is a part of Noah's family, and also Abraham, Isaac, and Jacob's. God had promised Abraham that someone would come from his family who would bless the whole world! Jesus' family includes Jesse, Jesse's son David, and David's son Solomon. God promised David that a king would come from his family who would rule forever. The prophet Isaiah said the Messiah would be born of a virgin. (Jesus' mother Mary was a virgin.)

Jesus came to earth as a baby in Bethlehem. God is Jesus' Father, but He chose Mary and Joseph to be Jesus' earthly parents. For many years, God had promised to send a Messiah to save people from sin. Jesus was God's plan to bring salvation to the world, and God had been working out His plan all along.

Christ connection

LEADER • The Old Testament prophets also said that Jesus would be the Son of God. Jesus did not use His status as God to make His life on earth easier. Jesus gave up His position in heaven, came to earth, and took on the form of a man.

Jesus did not stop being God the Son when He came to earth. ***Is Jesus God or a human? As the Son of God, Jesus is both fully God and fully human.***

Jesus had earthly parents, Mary and Joseph, but His true Father is God. Through Jesus, God kept His promises to Abraham and David. Jesus saves people from their sins and adopts them into God's family.

Tip: Use Scripture and the guide provided on page 13 to explain how to become a Christian. Make sure kids know when and where they can ask questions.

Questions from kids video (3 minutes)

Show the "Unit 19, Session 1" questions from kids video. Prompt kids to think about why Jesus is sometimes called "the last Adam." Guide them to discuss ways Jesus is greater than Adam.

· "Unit 19, Session 1" questions from kids video

 ## Missions moment (3 minutes)

LEADER • Let's take a quick trip together to Brazil. We'll visit a city called São Paulo, where missionaries

"São Paulo Presents" missions video
· world map

are sharing the gospel. **Jesus' family line proved He is the Messiah.** Missionaries want people all over the world to know Jesus, the Messiah.

Point out Brazil on a world map. Then play the video "São Paulo Presents." Close in prayer for the people of Brazil.

Key passage (5 minutes)

- Key Passage Poster
- "The Word Was God (John 1:1-2)" song

Show the key passage poster. Lead boys and girls to read together John 1:1-2.

LEADER • These are the first words John wrote in the Gospel of John. He introduces us to the Word. The Word is Jesus, God the Son. Let's work on memorizing John 1:1-2 over the next few weeks.

Lead kids in singing "The Word Was God (John 1:1-2)."

Sing (4 minutes)

- "Jesus Messiah" song
- Bible

Open your Bible and read aloud Galatians 4:4-5.

LEADER • When God sent His Son into the world, God was working out His good plan to rescue sinners! God sent Jesus into the world so that we could be free from sin and adopted into His family. Let's sing!

Sing together "Jesus Messiah."

Pray (2 minutes)

Invite kids to pray before dismissing to apply the story.

LEADER • Lord God, thank You for Your Word! You kept Your promises to Abraham and David, and You blessed the whole world by sending Your Son. Help us to tell others about Jesus—the most important Person in history. We love You. Amen.

Dismiss to apply the story

The Gospel: God's Plan for Me

Ask kids if they have ever heard the word *gospel*. Clarify that the word *gospel* means "good news." It is the message about Christ, the kingdom of God, and salvation. Use the following guide to share the gospel with kids.

God rules. Explain to kids that the Bible tells us God created everything, and He is in charge of everything. Invite a volunteer to read Genesis 1:1 from the Bible. Read Revelation 4:11 or Colossians 1:16-17 aloud and explain what these verses mean.

We sinned. Tell kids that since the time of Adam and Eve, everyone has chosen to disobey God. (Romans 3:23) The Bible calls this sin. Because God is holy, God cannot be around sin. Sin separates us from God and deserves God's punishment of death. (Romans 6:23)

God provided. Choose a child to read John 3:16 aloud. Say that God sent His Son, Jesus, the perfect solution to our sin problem, to rescue us from the punishment we deserve. It's something we, as sinners, could never earn on our own. Jesus alone saves us. Read and explain Ephesians 2:8-9.

Jesus gives. Share with kids that Jesus lived a perfect life, died on the cross for our sins, and rose again. Because Jesus gave up His life for us, we can be welcomed into God's family for eternity. This is the best gift ever! Read Romans 5:8; 2 Corinthians 5:21; or 1 Peter 3:18.

We respond. Tell kids that they can respond to Jesus. Read Romans 10:9-10,13. Review these aspects of our response: Believe in your heart that Jesus alone saves you through what He's already done on the cross. Repent, turning from self and sin to Jesus. Tell God and others that your faith is in Jesus.

Offer to talk with any child who is interested in responding to Jesus. Provide *I'm a Christian Now!* for new Christians to take home and complete with their families.

APPLY the Story

SESSION TITLE: From Adam to Jesus

BIBLE PASSAGE: Matthew 1; Luke 3; John 1

STORY POINT: Jesus' family line proved He is the Messiah.

KEY PASSAGE: John 1:1-2

BIG PICTURE QUESTION: Is Jesus God or a human? As the Son of God, Jesus is both fully God and fully human.

Key passage activity (5 minutes)

· Key Passage Poster
· dry erase board
· eraser
· marker

Display the key passage poster. Lead kids in reading aloud John 1:1-2 together. Write the words of the key passage on a dry erase board. Invite a volunteer to erase one word from the passage. Then challenge kids to say the key passage, filling in the missing word. Choose another volunteer to erase another word. Continue erasing words one at a time until kids can recite the entire key passage from memory.

SAY • Memorizing God's Word helps us remember what is true about God and about ourselves. Our key passage tells us that Jesus is the Word, and He has always existed. Jesus is God the Son. Keep working this week to memorize John 1:1-2. Next time, we'll see who remembers our key passage.

Discussion & Bible skills (10 minutes)

· Bibles, 1 per kid
· Story Point Poster
· Small Group Timeline and Map Set (005802970)
· Giant Timeline and Family Line of Jesus Posters (005802967)

Distribute Bibles. Guide boys and girls to open their Bibles to Matthew 1. Point out that the Book of Matthew is the first book in the New Testament and the first book of the four Gospels—Matthew, Mark, Luke, and John. Explain that the Gospels tell the story of Jesus' life, death, and resurrection. Choose a volunteer to read Matthew 1:1.

SAY • The first words in the New Testament show that
God kept the promise He made throughout the
Old Testament. Since sin entered the world, God
promised to send a Rescuer.

Tip: Show kids the
family line of Jesus
poster and point
out Abraham and
David.

God said this Savior would come from the family
of Abraham (Gen. 22:18) and the family of King
David (Jer. 23:5). Jesus was called "the Son of David"
and "the Son of Abraham." **Jesus' family line proved
He is the Messiah.**

Ask the following questions. Lead the group to discuss:

Option: Retell or
review the Bible
story using the
bolded text of the
Bible story script.

1. What kinds of people are in Jesus' family line? *Invite
kids to share their observations. Point out that God uses
all types of people in His plans. God made Abraham a
father even in his old age. God used Jacob even though
he dressed in his brother's clothes to get a blessing meant
for Esau. Rahab hid the Israelite spies. Ruth was a
Moabite who followed her mother-in-law back to
Judah. David was a shepherd boy. Solomon asked for
wisdom. God made Josiah a king at 8 years old.*
(Option: Choose a volunteer to read Eph. 1:4-5.)

2. How is Jesus different than the other people in His
family line? *Emphasize that **as the Son of God, Jesus
is both fully God and fully human.** Unlike the other
people in His family line, Jesus never sinned.*
(Option: Choose a volunteer to read Heb. 4:15.)

3. What does it mean to be adopted into God's family?
*Lead kids to recognize that adoption describes our new
relationship with God. We gain all of the responsibilities
and privileges of being a child of God. God gives His
Spirit to lead His children. We live for Him, and we
will live with Him forever.*
(Option: Choose a volunteer to read Gal. 4:6-7.)

· map of your city or community
· online photos of city or state landmarks

Tip: Use this activity option to reinforce the missions moment from Teach the Story.

Activity choice (10 minutes)

OPTION 1: Check the map

SAY • In the video about São Paulo, we saw a few things that seem important to the people there: music, art, and food. What are some things that are important to our community? (*sports, food, theater, church, beach, and so on*) If someone new moved to our community, where should we take that person? [*Allow time for kids to answer.*]

If you have a city map or photos, show the kids and point out some of the landmarks. If you prefer, simply describe some landmarks or places in your community that kids may be familiar with, like a local park or favorite restaurant.

SAY • When missionaries move to a new city, they want to get to know the people and places. They learn about things like the local music and food because they want to make new friends. They will tell their friends about Jesus, the Messiah, so that more families will know about Him.

OPTION 2: Fully God, fully man

· "Attributes of God" printable
· Bibles

Option: Review the gospel with boys and girls. Explain that kids are welcome to speak with you or another teacher if they have questions.

Before the session, print and cut apart the "Attributes of God" cards. Hide the cards around the room. Challenge kids to find the cards and sort them into two categories— things that describe only God, and things that can describe God and people. As time allows, select kids to find and read the referenced Bible verses on the cards.

SAY • We saw today that **Jesus' family line proved He is the Messiah.** *Is Jesus God or a human? As the Son of God, Jesus is both fully God and fully human.* The traits that describe God alone are called *incommunicable attributes*—like eternal, all-knowing, holy, all-powerful, everywhere, sovereign, and unchanging.

We are made in God's image and can reflect some of His attributes—His *communicable attributes*—like truthful, loving, just, merciful, and good.

Jesus came to earth as a baby, and He had earthly parents. But Jesus' true Father is God. Jesus never stopped being God when He came to earth, but He fully took the form of a man.

Journal and prayer (5 minutes)

Distribute journal pages and pencils. Guide kids to think about and answer the questions listed on the page:

- What does this story teach me about God or the gospel?
- What does the story teach me about myself?
- Are there any commands in this story to obey? How are they for God's glory and my good?
- Are there any promises in this story to remember? How do they help me trust and love God?
- How does this story help me to live on mission better?

As kids journal, invite them to share their ideas. Then pray, praising God for working out His plan to send Jesus from the beginning—through many generations. Thank Him for loving and remembering His people.

As time allows, lead kids to complete "Family Line Matching" on the activity page. Kids should match each description to the correct person from Jesus' family line.

· pencils
· Journal Page
· "Family Line Matching" activity page, 1 per kid

Tip: Give parents this week's *Big Picture Cards for Families* to allow families to interact with the biblical content at home.

Unit 19 · Session 2
John Was Born

BIBLE PASSAGE:
Luke 1

STORY POINT:
John was born to prepare
the way for Jesus.

KEY PASSAGE:
John 1:1-2

BIG PICTURE QUESTION:
Is Jesus God or a human? As the
Son of God, Jesus is both fully God
and fully human.

INTRODUCE THE STORY	TEACH THE STORY	APPLY THE STORY
(10–15 MINUTES)	(25–30 MINUTES)	(25–30 MINUTES)
PAGE 22	**PAGE 24**	**PAGE 30**

Additional resources are available at gospelproject.com. For free training and session-by-session help, visit ministrygrid.com/gospelproject.

Older Kids Leader Guide
Unit 19 • Session 2

LEADER Bible Study

Some of the last words of the Lord recorded in the Old Testament are found in Malachi 4: "Look, I am going to send you the prophet Elijah … he will turn the hearts of fathers to their children and the hearts of children to their fathers" (vv. 5-6). The Book of Malachi was written more than 400 years before Jesus was born. For centuries, God's people did not hear from Him. They were back in their homeland but were subject to other ruling nations. Eventually, the Romans took over.

The Roman emperor installed Herod as a leader over Judea and surrounding regions such as Samaria and Galilee. To gain the people's favor, King Herod replaced Zerubbabel's temple in Jerusalem with a beautiful marble temple constructed by 10,000 workers. This was the temple in which Zechariah, a priest from the family of Abijah, served the Lord. This was the temple in which God, through the angel Gabriel, broke His silence after so many years.

Zechariah and his wife, Elizabeth, were both "righteous in God's sight" (Luke 1:6), living by faith in God's promise to send a Messiah. Like Abraham and Sarah in Genesis 18, they were getting along in years and did not have any children. Elizabeth's barrenness was a point of disgrace for her among the community (Luke 1:25) and God graciously answered this couple's prayers.

An angel appeared to Zechariah in the temple sanctuary and delivered good news: "Your prayer has been heard. Your wife Elizabeth will bear a son." Echoing Malachi's prophecy, the angel declared this son would "turn the hearts of fathers to their children" (Luke 1:17)

For his doubting, Zechariah was rendered mute until the promise came to pass. When John was born, Zechariah could speak again. He praised God and prophesied. John was born to prepare the way for Jesus. John would point people to Jesus, the Savior God promised.

The **BIBLE** Story

John Was Born
Luke 1

Zechariah and his wife, Elizabeth, were old and had no children. They lived outside of Jerusalem in the hill country and **did what was right.** Zechariah was a priest and at that time, King Herod ruled over Judea. **Twice a year, Zechariah went to the temple in Jerusalem to carry out his duties as a priest.** Many priests served in the temple. **One day, Zechariah was chosen to go into the sanctuary of the Lord and burn incense.** People gathered outside to pray, and Zechariah went inside the sanctuary. **Suddenly, an angel of the Lord appeared. Zechariah was terrified!**

"Do not be afraid, Zechariah," the angel said. **"God heard your prayer. Your wife will have a son, and you will name him John.** His birth will bring you joy. God will be with Him. The Holy Spirit will fill him even before he is born."

The angel said that John would help many people turn back to God. John would go ahead of the Lord and get people ready for His coming.

Zechariah asked the angel, "How can I know this will happen? I'm old, and my wife is old."

The angel said, "God sent me to tell you this good news. Because

you did not believe my words, you won't be able to speak until these things happen."

Zechariah left the temple. The people outside realized he had seen a vision and could not talk. When he was done serving in Jerusalem, **Zechariah went home to Elizabeth. In time, she became pregnant and gave birth to a son.** Her neighbors and relatives rejoiced.

Zechariah and Elizabeth named their son John. Suddenly, Zechariah could speak again. He began praising God. The people who lived nearby could tell that God was with John. **The Holy Spirit filled John. Zechariah praised God and told the people God's words: "God has come to help His people. He will save us through David's family. He will rescue us from our enemies."** Then he spoke to John: "And you will be called a prophet of the Most High. You will go before the Lord to prepare the way for Him."

The time had come. God was going to bring His light into the darkness of the world. Peace was coming for God's people.

John grew up and lived in the wilderness until God called him to get the people ready for Jesus.

Christ Connection: When Zechariah believed God's word, he praised God. John was born to prepare the way for Jesus. John would point people to Jesus, and they would praise God for keeping His promise to send the Savior.

Bible Storytelling Tips

- **Make eye contact:** As you tell the story, make eye contact with kids to draw them in. Pause at appropriate points to build anticipation when the angel appears to Zechariah.
- **Dress in costume:** Wear Bible times clothes as you tell the story. Act out the role of Zechariah.

Into the World

INTRODUCE the Story

SESSION TITLE: John Was Born

BIBLE PASSAGE: Luke 1

STORY POINT: John was born to prepare the way for Jesus.

KEY PASSAGE: John 1:1-2

BIG PICTURE QUESTION: Is Jesus God or a human? As the Son of God, Jesus is both fully God and fully human.

Welcome time

Greet each kid as he or she arrives. Use this time to collect the offering, fill out attendance sheets, and help new kids connect to your group. Prompt kids to share their routines for getting ready for school in the morning. What happens if they aren't ready on time?

Activity page (5 minutes)

- "His Name Is ..." activity page, 1 per kid
- pencils or markers

Invite kids to complete "His Name Is ... " on the activity page. Guide kids to complete the dot-to-dots to find the name of Zechariah's son.

SAY • What name did you discover? (*John*) The name *John* means "The Lord is gracious." He shows us grace—undeserved favor. Today we will hear a story from the Bible about a baby who was born long ago. An angel told a man named Zechariah to name his baby John.

LOW PREP

Session starter (10 minutes)

- hula hoops
- music

OPTION 1: Musical hoops

Arrange several hula hoops at the front of the room or in a circle. Invite kids to play a game similar to musical chairs, except kids should move when there is no music and find a hoop to put one foot inside when you begin playing music. Explain that more than one kid can use a hoop. Before stopping the music to play another round, remove one hoop. More kids will have to share the remaining hoops. Play until one hoop remains and all kids try to share it.

SAY • That was a different way to play musical chairs. You waited for me to break the silence by playing the music. When you think of our game, remember that 400 years passed between the end of the Old Testament and the beginning of the New Testament. In those years, God was silent. He did not speak directly to His people. But in today's Bible story, God broke the silence. We'll find out how.

OPTION 2: Before and after cards
Print and cut apart the "First and Second" cards. Mix up the cards and arrange them facedown on a table in a grid.

· "First and Second" printable

Invite kids to play a memory game, turning over two cards at a time to find cards that match as a set of first and second cards. Help kids determine if the cards form a pair. If so, the player keeps the cards and play continues. If not, the player turns the cards facedown again and play continues.

SAY • Malachi, the last prophet in the Old Testament, said that someone would come before Jesus. The person who would get people ready for Jesus was John! We will learn more about John today.

Transition to teach the story

TEACH the Story

SESSION TITLE: John Was Born

BIBLE PASSAGE: Luke 1

STORY POINT: John was born to prepare the way for Jesus.

KEY PASSAGE: John 1:1-2

BIG PICTURE QUESTION: Is Jesus God or a human? As the Son of God, Jesus is both fully God and fully human.

Countdown

· countdown video

Show the countdown video as you transition to teach the story. Set it to end as the session begins.

Introduce the session (3 minutes)

· leader attire
· camera
· backpack
· family photo album
· alphabet blocks

Tip: If you prefer not to use themed content or characters, adapt or omit this introduction.

[Leader enters carrying a camera and a backpack. The backpack contains a family photo album with baby photos and a Bible. Blocks that spell out JOHN are arranged on a table.]

LEADER • Hi there! I'm [*your name*], studio photographer. I have to tell you, I've taken pictures of people from age 0 to 99, but one of my favorite groups of people to photograph is new babies.

Earlier this week, I took photos for a family who recently welcomed a baby boy into their family. This might surprise you, but newborn babies are not that difficult to work with. They are really sleepy, so I can gently pose them with some special props their parents have chosen and they usually stay put for the perfect photo. [*Show some baby photos.*] In this last shoot, the parents brought some blocks that I set up to display the new baby's name: J-O-H-N. I haven't finished editing those photos yet.

[*Retrieve a Bible.*] I'm excited for you to hear a story today about a baby from the Bible. Can you guess what his name was? [*Allow kids to respond.*] His name was John! Let's get started.

Big picture question (1 minute)

LEADER • Does anyone remember our big picture question and answer? [*Allow kids to respond.*] That's right. *Is Jesus God or a human? As the Son of God, Jesus is both fully God and fully human.* God's plan to rescue sinners was for God the Son to become a human, live the perfect life we failed to live, and take the punishment we deserve for our sins by dying on the cross in our place. Keep our big picture question and answer in mind as we hear today's Bible story.

Giant timeline (1 minute)

Show the giant timeline. Point to individual Bible stories as you review.

· Giant Timeline

LEADER • Can anyone tell me whose family we learned about last week? Yes! We learned about Jesus' family. You can find stories about many of the people in Jesus' family throughout the Old Testament. God promised to send a Messiah from the Jewish people. The New Testament begins with God's keeping that promise.

Between the Book of Malachi (the last book in the Old Testament) and the Gospels (the first books in the New Testament) God was silent. He did not speak directly to His people for 400 years. A lot changed for God's people during that time. The rulers in Rome took over, and some people might

Into the World

have wondered if God forgot about His people. Did God forget? No! In today's Bible story, we will hear what God said when He finally broke the silence.

Tell the Bible story (10 minutes)

- Bibles
- "John Was Born" video
- Big Picture Question Poster
- Bible Story Picture Poster
- Story Point Poster

Open your Bible to Luke 1. Use the Bible storytelling tips on the Bible story page to help you tell the story, or show the Bible story video "John Was Born."

LEADER • Zechariah and his wife, Elizabeth, were old, and they did not have any children. Zechariah was doing his job as a priest in the temple when he saw an angel! The angel Gabriel told Zechariah that he and his wife were going to be parents!

Do you think Zechariah was excited? He probably was! Then Gabriel told Zechariah to name his son John. Maybe this news sounded too good to be true! Zechariah wasn't sure if he could believe the angel. Was Gabriel telling the truth? Wasn't Elizabeth too old to have a baby? [*Allow kids to respond.*] Gabriel told Zechariah that he wouldn't be able to talk until these words from God came true.

When Zechariah left the temple, he couldn't talk. He had to gesture with his hands to communicate. Elizabeth found out she was going to have a baby. She knew the baby was a gift from God.

God was planning for this baby to be a prophet. God's people had not heard from God since the prophet Malachi, but God had not forgotten His plan to save people from their sin. After 400 years of silence, how did God speak? Look at Luke 1:13. [*Allow kids to read the verse and respond.*]

John was born to prepare the way for Jesus.

John would grow up and remind people about the Messiah God had promised to send. John was going to get people ready to meet Jesus.

Christ connection

LEADER • God's people hadn't heard from God for 400 years, but God didn't forget His plan to save people from their sin. Zechariah believed God's word, and he praised God. **John was born to prepare the way for Jesus.** John would point people to Jesus, and they would praise God for keeping His promise to send the Savior.

Tip: Use Scripture and the guide provided on page 29 to explain how to become a Christian. Make sure kids know when and where they can ask questions.

Questions from kids video (3 minutes)

Show the "Unit 19, Session 2" questions from kids video. Prompt kids to think about angels. Guide them to discuss why God made angels. What message does God give us to share with the world? Choose a kid to read aloud 2 Corinthians 5:20-21.

- "Unit 19, Session 2" questions from kids video

 ## Missions moment (3 minutes)

LEADER • **John was born to prepare the way for Jesus.** Have you ever thought that you were born to prepare the way for people to know Jesus? God wants us, no matter our age, to love Jesus and tell other people about Him.

- "Relentless Love (Part 1)" missions video

We're going to hear from two missionaries in Brazil who are preparing the way for people in São Paulo to know about Jesus.

Show the "Relentless Love (Part 1)" missions video and pray for missionaries in Brazil.

Key passage (5 minutes)

- Key Passage Poster
- "The Word Was God (John 1:1-2)" song

Show the key passage poster. Lead the boys and girls to read together John 1:1-2.

LEADER • The Word was with God. Whoa. Did you know God has never been lonely? God created man to be in relationship with Him, but not because He needed a friend. God the Father, God the Son—who is the Word, and God the Spirit have always been together.

Lead kids in singing "The Word Was God (John 1:1-2)."

Sing (4 minutes)

- "Jesus Messiah" song
- Bible

Open your Bible and read aloud Malachi 3:1.

LEADER • Hundreds of years before John was born, the prophet Malachi said that a messenger would come to get people ready for the Messiah. John is the messenger that Malachi spoke of. **John was born to prepare the way for Jesus.** God kept His promise; He always keeps His promises! Let's sing.

Sing together "Jesus Messiah."

Pray (2 minutes)

Invite kids to pray before dismissing to apply the story.

LEADER • Lord God, You are good and Your plans are good. Thank You for giving us Your Word so we can know what is true about You and about ourselves. You gave Zechariah and Elizabeth a son in their old age to bring them joy and gladness. **John was born to prepare the way for Jesus**, who brings us joy and gladness by rescuing us from our sins. Help us share this joyful news with others! Amen.

Dismiss to apply the story

The Gospel: God's Plan for Me

Ask kids if they have ever heard the word *gospel*. Clarify that the word *gospel* means "good news." It is the message about Christ, the kingdom of God, and salvation. Use the following guide to share the gospel with kids.

God rules. Explain to kids that the Bible tells us God created everything, and He is in charge of everything. Invite a volunteer to read Genesis 1:1 from the Bible. Read Revelation 4:11 or Colossians 1:16-17 aloud and explain what these verses mean.

We sinned. Tell kids that since the time of Adam and Eve, everyone has chosen to disobey God. (Romans 3:23) The Bible calls this sin. Because God is holy, God cannot be around sin. Sin separates us from God and deserves God's punishment of death. (Romans 6:23)

God provided. Choose a child to read John 3:16 aloud. Say that God sent His Son, Jesus, the perfect solution to our sin problem, to rescue us from the punishment we deserve. It's something we, as sinners, could never earn on our own. Jesus alone saves us. Read and explain Ephesians 2:8-9.

Jesus gives. Share with kids that Jesus lived a perfect life, died on the cross for our sins, and rose again. Because Jesus gave up His life for us, we can be welcomed into God's family for eternity. This is the best gift ever! Read Romans 5:8; 2 Corinthians 5:21; or 1 Peter 3:18.

We respond. Tell kids that they can respond to Jesus. Read Romans 10:9-10,13. Review these aspects of our response: Believe in your heart that Jesus alone saves you through what He's already done on the cross. Repent, turning from self and sin to Jesus. Tell God and others that your faith is in Jesus.

Offer to talk with any child who is interested in responding to Jesus. Provide *I'm a Christian Now!* for new Christians to take home and complete with their families.

APPLY the Story

SESSION TITLE: John Was Born

BIBLE PASSAGE: Luke 1

STORY POINT: John was born to prepare the way for Jesus.

KEY PASSAGE: John 1:1-2

BIG PICTURE QUESTION: Is Jesus God or a human? As the Son of God, Jesus is both fully God and fully human.

Key passage activity (5 minutes)

- Key Passage Poster
- beanbag or foam ball

Instruct kids to stand in a circle. Display the key passage poster. Lead kids in reading John 1:1-2 aloud together.

Give one kid a beanbag or foam ball. Prompt him to say the first word of the key passage and then toss the beanbag to another player. That kid will say the next word, toss the beanbag to another player who will say the next word, and so on. Encourage kids to toss the beanbag to players who have not yet received it before a player gets a second turn.

For an added challenge, remove or cover the key passage poster so kids must say the key passage from memory.

SAY • Good work, everyone. Our key passage teaches us about Jesus, who is God the Son. He has always existed. **John was born to prepare the way for Jesus.** God the Father planned to send His Son to be the Savior of the world.

Discussion & Bible skills (10 minutes)

- Bibles, 1 per kid
- Story Point Poster
- Small Group Timeline and Map Set (005802970)

Distribute Bibles. Guide boys and girls to open their Bibles to Luke 1. Explain that the Book of Luke is the third book in the New Testament. Remind kids that Zechariah was at the temple in Jerusalem when an angel appeared to him.

[*Point to Jerusalem (H4) on the New Testament Israel Map.*]
Then choose a volunteer to read aloud Luke 1:16-17.

SAY • The angel Gabriel told Zechariah that his son, John,
would do some very important things: He would
help people turn back to God. John would go ahead
of the Lord and get people ready for Him. John
would lead people who were disobeying God to turn
back to God and follow Him. **John was born to
prepare the way for Jesus.**

Ask the following questions. Lead the group to discuss:

Option: Retell or
review the Bible
story using the
bolded text of the
Bible story script.

1. What did Zechariah do after his son was born?
*Prompt kids to recall that Zechariah named the baby
John, just as the angel commanded. Then he was able to
speak, and he prophesied about John, saying he would
go before the Lord and get people ready for Him.*
(Option: Choose a volunteer to read Luke 1:76-68.)

2. The name *John* means "the Lord is gracious." Where
do you see God's grace in the Bible story or in your
own life? *Encourage kids to give examples. Help them
recognize God's grace in giving a son to Zechariah and
Elizabeth. Guide them to consider undeserved favor
in their lives, especially the gracious gift of salvation
through Jesus.*
(Option: Choose a volunteer to read Ex. 34:6.)

3. In what ways can we get people ready for Jesus'
return? *Invite kids to share their ideas. Emphasize that
Jesus commanded all believers to make disciples among
the nations. (Matt. 28:19) We can all be involved by
telling others about Jesus in our own communities,
supporting missionaries through prayer or giving, or
obeying God's call to go to the nations.*
(Option: Choose a volunteer to read 1 Pet. 4:7-11.)

LOW PREP

· beanbags or small
  smooth stones, 5

Tip: Use this
activity option
to reinforce the
missions moment
from Teach the
Story.

Activity choice (10 minutes)

OPTION 1: Cinco Marias

Introduce the Brazilian game "Cinco Marias" (or "Five Marias"). The game is similar to jacks and is usually played with small, smooth stones. Scatter four beanbags on the floor. Invite a volunteer to throw one bag into the air, grab one bag from the floor, and catch the tossed bag before it lands. Repeat, trying to grab two bags from the floor, and so on. Allow time for every kid to have a turn.

After everyone has a chance to play, take the five beanbags and brainstorm as a group five ways to pray for missionaries. Place one bag on the floor for each prayer request and ask for a volunteer to say a prayer aloud.

SAY • It's fun to learn something about a different culture, like this game from Brazil. We can be a part of God's mission to reach the nations by learning and praying. We are helping to prepare the way for people to know and love Jesus.

· index cards
· marker

OPTION 2: Team charades

Before the session, write several actions on separate index cards. (Examples: *skateboarding, opening a gift, walking a dog, building a sandcastle, playing baseball*)

Form two teams of kids. Choose one player from each team to come to you, and discreetly show both of them a prepared word card. Both players may begin performing motions to help their teams guess the action. Instruct kids that they may not speak. Teams may call out their guesses. Award a point to the first team to guess correctly. Then choose two different players to perform the next action.

Option: Review the gospel with boys and girls. Explain that kids are welcome to speak with you or another teacher if they have questions.

SAY • Why was Zechariah unable to speak in today's Bible story? (*He did not believe the angel's message from*

God.) Zechariah believed God's word, and he praised God. **John was born to prepare the way for Jesus.** John would point people to Jesus, and they would praise God for keeping His promise to send the Savior.

Acting out a message is one way we can communicate besides talking. We can also write words, draw pictures, or use sign language. Think of someone you can share today's story with this week and then make time to tell that person!

Journal and prayer (5 minutes)

Distribute journal pages and pencils. Guide kids to think about and answer the questions listed on the page:

- What does this story teach me about God or the gospel?
- What does the story teach me about myself?
- Are there any commands in this story to obey? How are they for God's glory and my good?
- Are there any promises in this story to remember? How do they help me trust and love God?
- How does this story help me to live on mission better?

As kids journal, invite them to share their ideas. Then pray, praising God for the Bible and asking Him to help kids trust His Word. Thank Him for providing salvation through His Son, and ask Him for opportunities to serve others this week and show them the love of Jesus.

As time allows, lead kids to complete "Missing Words" on the activity page. Kids should fill in the blanks with the correct words from the word box.

· pencils
· Journal Page
· "Missing Words" activity page, 1 per kid

Tip: Give parents this week's *Big Picture Cards for Families* to allow families to interact with the biblical content at home.

Unit 19 · Session 3
Jesus Was Born

BIBLE PASSAGE:
Luke 2

STORY POINT:
Jesus was born to be God's
promised Savior.

KEY PASSAGE:
John 1:1-2

BIG PICTURE QUESTION:
Is Jesus God or a human?
As the Son of God, Jesus is both fully
God and fully human.

INTRODUCE THE STORY	TEACH THE STORY	APPLY THE STORY
(10–15 MINUTES)	(25–30 MINUTES)	(25–30 MINUTES)
PAGE 38	PAGE 40	PAGE 46

 → →

Additional resources are available at gospelproject.com. For free training and session-by-session help, visit ministrygrid.com/gospelproject.

LEADER Bible Study

After the angel Gabriel appeared to Zechariah and predicted the birth of John—the forerunner of the Messiah—he appeared to Mary and predicted that she too would have a baby. This baby would be named Jesus, and He would be God's Son. "He will be great and will be called the Son of the Most High … His kingdom will have no end," Gabriel said. (See Luke 1:32-33.) Mary visited Zechariah and his wife, Elizabeth, who was pregnant with John. Inside the womb, John leaped for joy in the presence of Mary's unborn baby.

Mary and Joseph lived in Nazareth. When Caesar Augustus called for a census, they traveled to Bethlehem—the very place the Messiah was prophesied to be born. (Micah 5:2) There, in a stable, God the Son entered the world as a baby.

Imagine the shepherds' surprise when an angel of the Lord suddenly appeared. The Bible says that they were terrified! But the angel brought them good news: "Today in the city of David a Savior was born for you, who is the Messiah, the Lord" (Luke 2:11). This Savior—the long-awaited deliverer and redeemer—had come.

Not only did Jesus come into the world as the Savior, He came as our King. Some time after Jesus' birth, wise men came to worship Jesus. They brought Him gifts suitable for a king—gold, frankincense, and myrrh. Jesus is the King who will rule forever, just as God promised King David. (See 2 Sam. 7.)

When you share this story with kids, remind them that Jesus came because we needed Him. The purpose of Jesus' birth was twofold: to bring glory to God and to make peace between God and those who trust in Jesus' death and resurrection. Celebrating the birth of Jesus is about rejoicing over the greatest gift we could ever receive. God's own Son came to earth to be our Savior and our King.

Jesus Was Born
Luke 2

Mary and Joseph lived in the town of **Nazareth. During the time Mary was pregnant, the Roman emperor,** Caesar Augustus, **announced that everyone needed to be registered** for a census.

Since **Joseph** was a descendant of King David, he **and Mary** traveled to **Bethlehem,** the city of David.

While they were there, the time came for Mary to have her baby. Mary and Joseph looked for a safe place to stay, but every place was full. So Mary and Joseph found a place where animals were kept, and that is where Mary had her baby. Joseph named Him Jesus. Mary wrapped the baby tightly in cloth and laid Him in a feeding trough.

That night, some shepherds were watching over their sheep in the fields near Bethlehem. Suddenly, an angel stood before them and the glory of the Lord shone around them. They were terrified! **The angel said,** "Don't be afraid! **I have very good news for you and for all the people: Today a Savior, who is the Messiah and the Lord, was born for you in the city of David."** Then the angel said, **"You will find a baby wrapped tightly in cloth and lying in a manger."**

Suddenly, a whole army of angels appeared, praising God and saying, "Glory to God in the highest heaven, and peace on earth to people He favors!"

When the angels left and returned to heaven, **the shepherds** decided to go see if the angel's words were true. They **hurried to Bethlehem and found Mary and Joseph and the baby, who was lying in the feeding trough. Then the shepherds went and told others about the baby Jesus.** Everyone who heard about Jesus was surprised and amazed. Mary thought about everything that was happening and tried to understand it. **The shepherds returned to their fields, praising God because everything had happened just as the angel said.**

Christ Connection: The birth of Jesus was good news! Jesus was not an ordinary baby. He is God's Son, sent to earth from heaven. Jesus, the promised Savior, came into the world to deliver us from sin and death.

Bible Storytelling Tips

- **Use props:** As you tell the story, display a nativity scene. Allow kids to move the pieces around as you tell the story.
- **Adjust lighting:** Dim the lights to simulate a nighttime setting. Shine a bright light when describing the angel's appearance.

INTRODUCE the Story

SESSION TITLE: Jesus Was Born
BIBLE PASSAGE: Luke 2
STORY POINT: Jesus was born to be God's promised Savior.
KEY PASSAGE: John 1:1-2
BIG PICTURE QUESTION: Is Jesus God or a human? As the Son of God, Jesus is both fully God and fully human.

Welcome time

Greet each kid as he or she arrives. Use this time to collect the offering, fill out attendance sheets, and help new kids connect to your group. Prompt kids to share about some of their responsibilities. Have they ever been responsible for something that seemed too difficult to accomplish?

Activity page (5 minutes)

· "Story Stars" activity page, 1 per kid
· pencils or markers

Invite kids to complete "Story Stars" on the activity page. Guide kids to find the words for the coordinate points and write out today's story point.

SAY • Today we are going to hear the story of Jesus' birth. Have you ever heard the story of how Jesus was born? [*Allow kids to respond.*] Today we will dive into the story of how Jesus was born and think more about why He was born.

Session starter (10 minutes)

LOW PREP

· paper
· crayons, markers, or colored pencils

OPTION 1: Becoming small
Form groups of two to four kids. Invite each group to choose a small animal (cat, hamster, ladybug, turtle, squirrel, and so on).

Guide them to choose one person in the group to draw a picture of the animal. One person should be the writer. Group members should discuss what it might be like to live as that animal. Prompt kids to write a journal entry from the perspective of the animal about their activities in a day. Encourage kids to write several sentences.

Choose volunteers to read the stories aloud and share their drawings.

SAY • Those were some interesting stories! I'm not sure I would like to be an animal for a day. It would definitely be a step down from everything I get to enjoy as a person. Have you ever thought about what it was like for God the Son to come down to earth as a man? Think about that as we hear our Bible story.

draw and write abt it

OPTION 2: Word list

Form two teams of kids. Give each team a piece of paper and a pencil. Instruct a player on each team to write the word *CHRISTMAS* vertically down the left side of the paper, one letter per line. On the right side of the paper, she should write it in the opposite way, starting at the bottom and writing up (one letter per line).

· paper
· pencils
· dictionary

Tip: If your group is small, form words all together.

Challenge teams to fill in between the letters to create new words. (Examples: CowS, HulA, RooM, InpuT, SeaS, TikI, MotoR, ArcH, SoniC) If teams get stuck as time runs out, allow kids to consult a dictionary.

SAY • What are some things you think of when you hear the word Christmas? [*Call on kids to share.*] Great answers. When we hear our Bible story today, see if you notice some of the words that were mentioned.

Transition to teach the story

TEACH the Story

SESSION TITLE: Jesus Was Born
BIBLE PASSAGE: Luke 2
STORY POINT: Jesus was born to be God's promised Savior.
KEY PASSAGE: John 1:1-2
BIG PICTURE QUESTION: Is Jesus God or a human? As the Son of God, Jesus is both fully God and fully human.

Countdown

· countdown video

Show the countdown video as you transition to teach the story. Set it to end as the session begins.

Introduce the session (3 minutes)

· leader attire
· camera
· backpack
· Bible
· alphabet blocks

Tip: If you prefer not to use themed content or characters, adapt or omit this introduction.

[Leader enters carrying a camera and a backpack. The backpack contains a family photo album with baby photos and a Bible. Blocks that spell out JESUS are arranged on a table.]

LEADER • Hi there! I am so glad to see you. In case you forgot, my name is *[your name]*, and I am a studio photographer. Last week I told you about some photos I took of a new baby named John. I just got an exciting call yesterday from one of his relatives asking me to schedule another baby photo shoot— not for John but for his cousin who was just born. I remember spending a lot of summers with a cousin who was just a bit older than me. Those boys are going to have so much fun growing up together.

[*Retrieve a Bible.*] I'm excited to share today's Bible story with you. It's about the birth of John's cousin Jesus. Let's get started.

Big picture question (1 minute)

LEADER • Here's our big picture question and answer: *Is Jesus God or a human? As the Son of God, Jesus is both fully God and fully human.*

Now I'll ask the question, and you say the answer. *Is Jesus God or a human?* [*Pause for kids to respond.*] *As the Son of God, Jesus is both fully God and fully human.*

God the Son became a human, lived the perfect life we failed to live, and took the punishment we deserve for our sins by dying on the cross in our place. Think about that as you listen to today's Bible story.

Giant timeline (1 minute)

Show the giant timeline. Point to individual Bible stories as you review.

· Giant Timeline

LEADER • The stories we've heard the last couple of weeks were about Jesus' family and the birth of John. **Jesus' family line proved He is the Messiah. John was born to prepare the way for Jesus.**

Does anyone remember what part of the Bible these stories are found in? (*New Testament, Gospels*) The Bible story we will hear today is called "Jesus Was Born." Whether this is your first time hearing this story or your one hundredth time, there is always something new to learn in God's Word.

· Bibles
· "Jesus Was Born" video
· Big Picture Question Poster
· Bible Story Picture Poster
· Story Point Poster

Tell the Bible story (10 minutes)

Open your Bible to Luke 2. Use the Bible storytelling tips on the Bible story page to help you tell the story, or show the Bible story video "Jesus Was Born."

LEADER • Incredible! Can you imagine what it was like to travel from Nazareth to Bethlehem? The journey for Mary and Joseph was long—about 90 miles, and cars hadn't been invented yet! When they got there, Mary needed a safe place to have her baby. Imagine knocking on doors to find a place to stay, only to discover that every place was already full. So Mary and Joseph went to a place where animals were kept and that is where Jesus was born.

Do you know why Mary's baby was called Jesus? Look at Matthew 1:21. [*Allow kids to read the verse and respond.*] The name *Jesus* means "Savior."

Imagine being a shepherd in the dark hills when an angel appeared, the glory of the Lord shining all around. The shepherds were terrified. Do you remember what the angel said to them? Look at Luke 2:10-12. [*Allow kids to read and respond.*]

The shepherds hurried to Bethlehem and found the baby. What did the shepherds do after they saw Baby Jesus? Look at Luke 2:20. [*Allow kids to read the verse and respond.*]

We too can tell others the good news: **Jesus was born to be God's promised Savior!**

Christ connection

Tip: Use Scripture and the guide provided on page 45 to explain how to become a Christian. Make sure kids know when and where they can ask questions.

LEADER • The birth of Jesus was good news! Jesus was not an ordinary baby. He is God's Son, sent to earth from heaven. So, *is Jesus God or a human? As the Son of God, Jesus is both fully God and fully human.* Jesus, the promised Savior, came into the world to deliver us from sin and death.

Questions from kids video (3 minutes)

Show the "Unit 19, Session 3" questions from kids video. Prompt kids to think about who Jesus is. Guide them to discuss how we know Jesus really is the promised Messiah.

· "Unit 19, Session 3" questions from kids video

Missions moment (3 minutes)

Display the Brazilian flag and distribute the Brazil facts among five volunteers. Instruct them to take turns reading the facts, pausing when they get to the blank so other kids can call out the word they think fits in the blank.

· "Brazilian Flag" printable
· "Brazil Facts" printable

LEADER • **Jesus was born to be God's promised Savior.** That's what missionaries want people all over the world to know. The Bible teaches us that we should go and tell all people about the Savior. That's why missionaries go to places like Brazil.

Close in prayer, thanking God for missionaries.

Key passage (5 minutes)

Show the key passage poster. Lead the boys and girls to read together John 1:1-2.

· Key Passage Poster
· "The Word Was God (John 1:1-2)" song

LEADER • As we celebrate Jesus' birth, think about the miracle of God's coming to earth as a man. Jesus' birth wasn't His beginning. No one created Jesus. The Bible says God the Son has always existed. He was with God, and He is God. He became a human—Jesus—and lived on earth. God came down to be with us and to rescue us. Let's sing.

Lead kids in singing "The Word Was God (John 1:1-2)."

Sing (4 minutes)

Open your Bible and read aloud James 1:17.

· "Jesus Messiah" song
· Bible

LEADER • Every good and perfect gift comes from God.

Into the World

Jesus is God's gift of salvation to His people! In Luke 2, the angel announced that Jesus would bring great joy. Let's sing to Jesus, our Savior and King! Sing together "Jesus Messiah."

Pray (2 minutes)

Invite kids to pray before dismissing to apply the story.

LEADER • Lord, we echo the words of the angels in the fields: Glory to God in the highest heaven! You were working out Your perfect plan to save sinners when You sent Your Son into the world as a helpless baby at just the right time. We praise Jesus as the Prince of Peace and look to Him as a light shining in a dark world. What a gift! We love You. Amen.

Dismiss to apply the story

The Gospel: God's Plan for Me

Ask kids if they have ever heard the word *gospel*. Clarify that the word *gospel* means "good news." It is the message about Christ, the kingdom of God, and salvation. Use the following guide to share the gospel with kids.

God rules. Explain to kids that the Bible tells us God created everything, and He is in charge of everything. Invite a volunteer to read Genesis 1:1 from the Bible. Read Revelation 4:11 or Colossians 1:16-17 aloud and explain what these verses mean.

We sinned. Tell kids that since the time of Adam and Eve, everyone has chosen to disobey God. (Romans 3:23) The Bible calls this sin. Because God is holy, God cannot be around sin. Sin separates us from God and deserves God's punishment of death. (Romans 6:23)

God provided. Choose a child to read John 3:16 aloud. Say that God sent His Son, Jesus, the perfect solution to our sin problem, to rescue us from the punishment we deserve. It's something we, as sinners, could never earn on our own. Jesus alone saves us. Read and explain Ephesians 2:8-9.

Jesus gives. Share with kids that Jesus lived a perfect life, died on the cross for our sins, and rose again. Because Jesus gave up His life for us, we can be welcomed into God's family for eternity. This is the best gift ever! Read Romans 5:8; 2 Corinthians 5:21; or 1 Peter 3:18.

We respond. Tell kids that they can respond to Jesus. Read Romans 10:9-10,13. Review these aspects of our response: Believe in your heart that Jesus alone saves you through what He's already done on the cross. Repent, turning from self and sin to Jesus. Tell God and others that your faith is in Jesus.

Offer to talk with any child who is interested in responding to Jesus. Provide *I'm a Christian Now!* for new Christians to take home and complete with their families.

APPLY the Story

SESSION TITLE: Jesus Was Born
BIBLE PASSAGE: Luke 2
STORY POINT: Jesus was born to be God's promised Savior.
KEY PASSAGE: John 1:1-2
BIG PICTURE QUESTION: Is Jesus God or a human? As the Son of God, Jesus is both fully God and fully human.

Key passage activity (5 minutes)

· Key Passage Poster
· construction paper
· markers
· scissors
· ziplock bags

Display the key passage poster. Lead kids in reading aloud John 1:1-2 together. Give each kid a piece of paper and a marker. Instruct kids to write the key passage, filling up as much of the paper as they can. Then provide scissors and invite them cut their papers into puzzle pieces.

Direct kids to mix up their puzzle pieces and assemble them to practice saying the key passage. If time allows, let kids trade and complete a partner's puzzle. Provide ziplock bags for kids to take home the puzzles.

SAY • What does our key passage tell us about God the Son? [*Allow kids to respond.*] Jesus was no ordinary baby. He is God the Son who came to earth as a human. Let's say our big picture question and answer: ***Is Jesus God or a human? As the Son of God, Jesus is both fully God and fully human.***

Discussion & Bible skills (10 minutes)

· Bibles, 1 per kid
· Story Point Poster
· Small Group Timeline and Map Set
  (005802970)

Distribute Bibles. Guide boys and girls to open their Bibles to Luke 2. Explain that the Book of Luke was written by a doctor named Luke. Point out that in today's Bible story, Joseph and Mary traveled from their home in Nazareth to the town of Bethlehem. [*Help kids locate Nazareth (E5) and Bethlehem (I4) on the New Testament Israel Map.*] Then choose a volunteer to read aloud Luke 2:10-11.

SAY • Jesus' birth was good news! Jesus wasn't born into the world to just show people the right way to live or be kind to people; **Jesus was born to be God's promised Savior.** A *savior* is someone who saves from danger or destruction. Jesus was born to rescue sinners from sin and death.

Ask the following questions. Lead the group to discuss:

1. Why do you think Jesus was born in such a humble way rather than in a palace to a wealthy family? *Guide kids to consider how Jesus can relate to ordinary people because of His upbringing. He gave up His glory and power in heaven to live humbly among people. Jesus' birth reflects how His kingdom's values differ from the world's values. We can boldly and humbly approach His throne in prayer.*
(Option: Choose a volunteer to read Heb. 4:15-16.)

2. Why was Jesus' birth good news? *Help kids understand that Jesus came because we needed Him. God showed His love for us by sending His Son into the world. We were separated from God because of our sins, but God was working out His promise to rescue sinners through the life, death, and resurrection of Jesus.*
(Option: Choose a volunteer to read John 3:16.)

3. Why should we tell others about Jesus? *Lead kids to recognize that salvation through Jesus bring the privilege and responsibility of sharing the gospel with the world. God calls us to live as witnesses to the saving power of Jesus—in what we say and how we live.*
(Option: Choose a volunteer to read Ps. 66:16.)

Option: Retell or review the Bible story using the bolded text of the Bible story script.

Activity choice (10 minutes)

OPTION 1: String beads

SAY • Arts and crafts are very popular in Brazil. Many artists enjoy painting, making things out of clay, weaving baskets, and making colorful jewelry. Beaded jewelry is common and is often sold in markets.

Invite kids to make a beaded bracelet or necklace using the beads and string or yarn. Let them choose their colors and patterns, and then string the beads. Help them tie a knot to finish the necklace or bracelet. Encourage kids to give the jewelry they made to someone and tell that person that Jesus is the Lord and Savior.

If time permits, allow them to make a piece of jewelry to keep. As they work, remind them of missionaries in Brazil who tell artists and craftsmen about Jesus.

OPTION 2: Make a blanket

Invite kids to follow these steps to make a blanket. If class time is limited, complete steps 1 to 3 before the session and allow kids to compete the blankets by knotting the fringe.

1. Cut off the finished edge of two pieces of fleece fabric. Trim the pieces if necessary to ensure they are the same size.

2. Lay the pieces together. Cut 5-inch squares from each corner.

3. Every inch around the blanket, cut a 5-inch slit.

4. Demonstrate how to pick up two layers of fringe and knot them together.

Give the blanket along with a small picture book to a family in your church with a new baby. If your group is large, consider making multiple blankets.

Older Kids Leader Guide
Unit 19 • Session 3

SAY • When Jesus was born, Mary wrapped Him tightly in cloth. The birth of Jesus was good news! Jesus came because we needed Him. Jesus was no ordinary baby; **Jesus was born to be God's promised Savior!** *Is Jesus God or a human? As the Son of God, Jesus is both fully God and fully human.* He is the greatest gift we could ever receive. God's own Son came to earth to be our Savior and our King.

Option: Review the gospel with boys and girls. Explain that kids are welcome to speak with you or another teacher if they have questions.

Journal and prayer (5 minutes)

Distribute journal pages and pencils. Guide kids to think about and answer the questions listed on the page:

- pencils
- Journal Page
- "True or False?" activity page, 1 per kid

- What does this story teach me about God or the gospel?
- What does the story teach me about myself?
- Are there any commands in this story to obey? How are they for God's glory and my good?
- Are there any promises in this story to remember? How do they help me trust and love God?
- How does this story help me to live on mission better?

As kids journal, invite them to share their ideas. Then pray, thanking God for the greatest gift—His Son.

As time allows, lead kids to complete "True or False?" on the activity page. Kids should mark whether each statement is true or false and then correct any false statements.

Tip: Give parents this week's *Big Picture Cards for Families* to allow families to interact with the biblical content at home.

Unit 19 · Session 4
Jesus Was Dedicated

BIBLE PASSAGE:
Luke 2

STORY POINT:
Simeon and Anna worshiped Jesus as the Messiah.

KEY PASSAGE:
John 1:1-2

BIG PICTURE QUESTION:
Is Jesus God or a human?
As the Son of God, Jesus is both fully God and fully human.

INTRODUCE THE STORY (10–15 MINUTES) PAGE 54		**TEACH THE STORY** (25–30 MINUTES) PAGE 56		**APPLY THE STORY** (25–30 MINUTES) PAGE 62
	→		→	

Additional resources are available at gospelproject.com. For free training and session-by-session help, visit ministrygrid.com/gospelproject.

LEADER Bible Study

God had chosen Mary and Joseph to be Jesus' earthly parents. Mary and Joseph named their baby Jesus, obeying God in faith that salvation had indeed come into the world. (See Matt. 1:21.) When the time came for Jesus to be dedicated and Mary to be purified, Mary and Joseph took Jesus to the temple in Jerusalem.

According to the law given to Moses, after a woman gave birth, she was "unclean" and would observe a period of purification. Then she would bring an offering to the priest. (See Lev. 12:1-6.) Jesus was about five weeks old when Mary and Joseph dedicated Him to the Lord and offered the required sacrifice.

Simeon was also at the temple that day, not by mere coincidence but by the Holy Spirit's leading. (Luke 2:27) Simeon spent His life serving the Lord and looked forward to the day when God would keep His promise to comfort Israel. (See Isa. 57:18.) God promised that Simeon would live long enough to see the Messiah. That day had finally come. Imagine his joy. At last, the Savior was here!

Simeon saw the baby Jesus, took Him in his arms, and praised God. Simeon expressed prophetic praise, trusting by faith that God would keep His promise through this child: "My eyes have seen your salvation" (Luke 2:30). Through Jesus, everyone would be able to see God's plan. Jesus would be a light for all the nations. He would bring honor to Israel.

Anna, a prophetess, also praised too. At well over a hundred years old, Anna began to speak about Jesus to everyone who was looking forward to God's bringing salvation to His people.

Today, we can have faith in Jesus and His finished work on the cross for our salvation. When God opens our eyes to the good news of the gospel, we can live and die in peace, for our eyes have seen His salvation. We can joyfully share this good news with others.

The **BIBLE** Story

Jesus Was Dedicated
Luke 2

Mary and Joseph's baby—God's own Son—was a few days old when Mary and Joseph named Him Jesus, just like the angel had told them to do. **One day, when Jesus was a few weeks old, Mary and Joseph took Jesus to the temple in Jerusalem.**

Mary and Joseph wanted to obey God and His law. The law that God gave Moses said, "When a woman's first son is born, his parents must dedicate him to the Lord." The law also said that the child's parents should give a sacrifice. **At the temple, Mary and Joseph presented Jesus to the Lord and offered two birds as a sacrifice.**

Another man was at the temple. His name was Simeon. Simeon loved God, and He trusted in God's promise to send a Messiah to save people from sin. **God's Spirit was with Simeon, and God had told Simeon that he would not die until he saw the One who would rescue people from their sin.**

That day, God's Spirit had led Simeon to the temple. **Simeon saw Jesus and picked Him up in his arms.** God's Spirit showed Simeon that Jesus was the promised Messiah. Simeon was so happy. He praised God and said, "Lord, you can let me die now. You kept Your promise, and I have seen the One who will save people from sin." **Simeon said that Jesus would save God's people, the Israelites, and Jesus would also save people from other nations.**

Mary and Joseph were amazed at what Simeon said. Simeon blessed Mary and Joseph. He told Mary that being Jesus' mother would be a very good thing, but it would also be very hard. Some people would love Jesus, but others would hate Him. Things were going to happen that would make Mary very sad.

A woman named Anna was at the temple too. Anna's husband had died, and Anna was very old. She stayed at the temple and worshiped God all the time. **Anna came up to Simeon, Jesus, Mary, and Joseph and she began to thank God. Anna talked about Jesus to people who were waiting for God to keep His promise to send a Savior. She told them the good news: the Savior was here!**

Mary and Joseph finished dedicating Jesus and making sacrifices to God. They obeyed God's law. Then they went back home to Nazareth. **Jesus grew up and was strong and healthy. He was wise, and God was happy with Him.**

Christ Connection: Throughout the Old Testament, God promised the arrival of a king who would redeem people. When Jesus arrived, Simeon and Anna knew He was the promised Messiah. Today, we have faith that Jesus is God's Son. We can trust Jesus for our salvation, and like Simeon and Anna, we should share the good news.

Bible Storytelling Tips

• **Act it out:** Choose four volunteers to silently act out the story as you tell it. Provide a baby doll as the baby Jesus.

• **Use hand gestures:** Capture kids' attention by moving your hands as you tell the story. Raise them as Simeon speaks or hold them to your head like Jesus' amazed parents.

INTRODUCE the Story

SESSION TITLE: Jesus Was Dedicated
BIBLE PASSAGE: Luke 2
STORY POINT: Simeon and Anna worshiped Jesus as the Messiah.
KEY PASSAGE: John 1:1-2
BIG PICTURE QUESTION: Is Jesus God or a human? As the Son of God, Jesus is both fully God and fully human.

Welcome time

Greet each kid as he or she arrives. Use this time to collect the offering, fill out attendance sheets, and help new kids connect to your group. Prompt kids to describe a time in the last week or so that they received good news. What was the news? Did they share the news with anyone? Why?

Activity page (5 minutes)

- "Seeing for Yourself" activity page, 1 per kid
- pencils or markers

Invite kids to complete "Seeing for Yourself" on the activity page. Guide kids to read the clues and cross out the words to discover Simeon's message.

SAY • Simeon was a man living in Jerusalem. He went to the temple and looked forward to the day God would bring salvation to the world. In today's Bible story, Simeon realized God had kept His promise. Let's find out more.

LOW PREP

Session starter (10 minutes)

OPTION 1: "My eyes have seen …" game
Invite kids to play a guessing game. Choose one player to lead. The leader should pick something in the room that is visible to everyone. He should say, "My eyes have seen … "

and then he should give a hint. For example, "My eyes have seen something that starts with the letter *P*." Or "My eyes have seen something green."

Kids should try to guess what the leader has spotted. When a player guesses correctly, she gets to be the new leader. Make sure every kid has a turn to lead.

SAY • In the Bible story we will hear today, a man named Simeon was waiting for something. When he finally saw what he was waiting for, Simeon said, "My eyes have seen Your salvation!" We'll find out what Simeon saw.

OPTION 2: Blanket drop game

Choose two volunteers to be blanket holders. Form two teams with the remaining kids. Give the volunteers a large sheet or blanket, and instruct them to hold it between them with one edge touching the ground to form a curtain of sorts. Instruct one team to sit on one side of the blanket and the other team to sit on the other side. Explain that you will choose a kid from each team to stand close to the blanket.

· large sheet or blanket

When you say "go," the volunteers will drop the blanket. The first standing player to recognize and shout the name of the other standing player earns a point for her team. Play additional rounds with other kids.

SAY • Great job! You had to be quick to remember a name for the face you saw. Sometimes recognizing even the people you see frequently can be difficult! With the help of the Holy Spirit, Simeon recognized someone he had never seen before.

Transition to teach the story

TEACH the Story

SESSION TITLE: Jesus Was Dedicated
BIBLE PASSAGE: Luke 2
STORY POINT: Simeon and Anna worshiped Jesus as the Messiah.
KEY PASSAGE: John 1:1-2
BIG PICTURE QUESTION: Is Jesus God or a human? As the Son of God, Jesus is both fully God and fully human.

Countdown

· countdown video

Show the countdown video as you transition to teach the story. Set it to end as the session begins.

Introduce the session (3 minutes)

· leader attire
· camera
· backpack
· family photo album
· Bible

Tip: If you prefer not to use themed content or characters, adapt or omit this introduction.

[Leader enters carrying a camera and a backpack. The backpack contains a family photo album and a Bible.]

LEADER • Hi, everyone! It's good to see you. My name is *[your name]*, and I'm a studio photographer. I've been taking a lot of photos of newborn babies lately. But a really fun part of my job is continuing to take photos of people as they grow. Usually families come in for photos once or twice a year plus any time they want to commemorate a special event. I've taken portraits of people in wedding dresses, graduation gowns, soccer jerseys, and business attire. Are there any special events in your life that have stood out as particularly memorable?

[Retrieve a Bible.] I'm excited to share today's Bible story with you. It's about a special event in Jesus' life—His dedication. Let's find out what happened.

Big picture question (1 minute)

LEADER • Here's our big picture question: *Is Jesus God or a human?* Does anyone remember the answer? [*Allow volunteers to say the answer.*] *As the Son of God, Jesus is both fully God and fully human.* The Bible says that Jesus is equal with God. And like us, Jesus experienced hunger, thirst, weariness, sorrow, and pain. As we keep learning about Jesus, keep in mind that *as the Son of God, Jesus is both fully God and fully human.*

Giant timeline (1 minute)

Show the giant timeline. Point to individual Bible stories as you review.

· Giant Timeline

LEADER • In the Bible story we are going to hear today, Jesus was still a baby. Let's review what we've learned about Jesus so far. First, we learned about Jesus' family. **Jesus' family line proved He is the Messiah.** Before Jesus came into the world, John was born. God had a plan for John's life. **John was born to prepare the way for Jesus.** Then, at just the right time, Jesus was born. Why was Jesus born? **Jesus was born to be God's promised Savior.**

When Jesus was about five weeks old, His earthly parents—Mary and Joseph—took Him to the temple to be dedicated. That's our Bible story today: "Jesus Was Dedicated."

Tell the Bible story (10 minutes)

Open your Bible to Luke 2. Use the Bible storytelling tips on the Bible story page to help you tell the story, or show the Bible story video "Jesus Was Dedicated."

· Bibles
· "Jesus Was Dedicated" video
· Big Picture Question Poster
· Bible Story Picture Poster
· Story Point Poster

LEADER • Jesus was still a small baby when Mary and Joseph took Him to Jerusalem. You see, God's law in the Old Testament said that every firstborn male was to be dedicated to the Lord. [*Choose a volunteer to read aloud Ex. 13:2,12.*] Mary and Joseph wanted to obey God's law, so they took Jesus to the temple to be dedicated.

Simeon was already at the temple. How did Simeon know Jesus would be there? Look at Luke 2:26-27. [*Allow kids to read the verses and respond.*] The Holy Spirit led Simeon to the temple. Simeon had been waiting for God to keep His promise to rescue His people from sin. In fact, God had revealed to Simeon that Simeon would see the Messiah in his lifetime. That day had finally come! Simeon took Jesus in his arms and praised God.

Who else was in the temple that day? Look at Luke 2:36. [*Allow kids to read the verse and respond.*] Anna had spent most of her life in the temple— serving God, fasting, and praying. She was more than 100 years old! **Simeon and Anna worshiped Jesus as the Messiah.** Then Anna told others about Him.

Christ connection

Tip: Use Scripture and the guide provided on page 61 to explain how to become a Christian. Make sure kids know when and where they can ask questions.

LEADER • Throughout the Old Testament, God promised the arrival of a king who would redeem people. When Jesus arrived, Simeon and Anna knew He was the promised Messiah.

Today, we have faith that Jesus is God's Son. God opens our eyes to the gospel. We can trust Jesus for our salvation, and like Simeon and Anna, we can joyfully share the good news with others.

Questions from kids video (3 minutes)

Show the "Unit 19, Session 4" questions from kids video. Prompt kids to think about Simeon and Anna's reaction to seeing Jesus. Guide them to discuss what they think it will be like when Jesus comes back to earth.

· "Unit 19, Session 4" questions from kids video

 ## Missions moment (3 minutes)

LEADER • We have been learning about missionaries in Brazil. In a previous video, we met missionaries Brandi and Amanda. They want people in Brazil to know Jesus personally and to worship Him, like **Simeon and Anna worshiped Jesus as the Messiah.** Let's watch what happened when a young woman, also named Amanda, decided that she needed Jesus.

· "Relentless Love (Part 2)" missions video

Play the "Relentless Love (Part 2)" missions video. Then pray for Amanda and other new believers in Brazil.

Key passage (5 minutes)

Show the key passage poster. Lead the boys and girls to read together John 1:1-2.

· Key Passage Poster
· "The Word Was God (John 1:1-2)" song

LEADER • Our key passage talks about God's Son as the Word. We can know more about someone when they share their words with us. They can talk about themselves or write down some things about themselves. We communicate through words.

God communicated Himself to the world through a living Word—Jesus! Through Jesus, we can know God and join His kingdom as adopted sons and daughters. Let's sing.

Lead kids in singing "The Word Was God (John 1:1-2)."

· "Jesus Messiah" song
· Bible

Sing (4 minutes)

Open your Bible and read aloud Psalm 62:1-2.

LEADER • In today's Bible story, **Simeon and Anna worshiped Jesus as the Messiah.** Simeon saw that God had kept His promise to send someone who would save people from sin. Salvation comes from God. We are not saved by doing good works but by trusting in Him alone. Let's sing.

Sing together "Jesus Messiah."

Pray (2 minutes)

Invite kids to pray before dismissing to apply the story.

LEADER • God, thank You for always keeping Your promises. The news that Jesus came to save people from sin is such good news. We confess that we do not always keep our promises, but You, Lord, are faithful. Help us trust in Jesus for our salvation. Amen.

Dismiss to apply the story

The Gospel: God's Plan for Me

Ask kids if they have ever heard the word *gospel*. Clarify that the word *gospel* means "good news." It is the message about Christ, the kingdom of God, and salvation. Use the following guide to share the gospel with kids.

God rules. Explain to kids that the Bible tells us God created everything, and He is in charge of everything. Invite a volunteer to read Genesis 1:1 from the Bible. Read Revelation 4:11 or Colossians 1:16-17 aloud and explain what these verses mean.

We sinned. Tell kids that since the time of Adam and Eve, everyone has chosen to disobey God. (Romans 3:23) The Bible calls this sin. Because God is holy, God cannot be around sin. Sin separates us from God and deserves God's punishment of death. (Romans 6:23)

God provided. Choose a child to read John 3:16 aloud. Say that God sent His Son, Jesus, the perfect solution to our sin problem, to rescue us from the punishment we deserve. It's something we, as sinners, could never earn on our own. Jesus alone saves us. Read and explain Ephesians 2:8-9.

Jesus gives. Share with kids that Jesus lived a perfect life, died on the cross for our sins, and rose again. Because Jesus gave up His life for us, we can be welcomed into God's family for eternity. This is the best gift ever! Read Romans 5:8; 2 Corinthians 5:21; or 1 Peter 3:18.

We respond. Tell kids that they can respond to Jesus. Read Romans 10:9-10,13. Review these aspects of our response: Believe in your heart that Jesus alone saves you through what He's already done on the cross. Repent, turning from self and sin to Jesus. Tell God and others that your faith is in Jesus.

Offer to talk with any child who is interested in responding to Jesus. Provide *I'm a Christian Now!* for new Christians to take home and complete with their families.

APPLY the Story

SESSION TITLE: Jesus Was Dedicated

BIBLE PASSAGE: Luke 2

STORY POINT: Simeon and Anna worshiped Jesus as the Messiah.

KEY PASSAGE: John 1:1-2

BIG PICTURE QUESTION: Is Jesus God or a human? As the Son of God, Jesus is both fully God and fully human.

Key passage activity (5 minutes)

- Key Passage Poster
- index cards
- marker

Before the session, write the words of the key passage on separate index cards. Mix up the cards. Display the key passage poster. Lead kids in reading John 1:1-2 aloud.

Distribute the prepared key passage cards. Challenge kids to arrange the cards in the correct order. When kids finish, lead them to read the key passage together.

If time allows, mix up the cards and play again. For an added challenge, include word cards that are not part of the key passage and instruct kids to find and remove words that do not belong.

SAY • Does anyone want to say our key passage from memory? [*Invite volunteers to recite John 1:1-2.*] Our key passage reminds us that Jesus—God the Son—has always existed. No one created Him. Before He came to earth, God the Son was in heaven. All along, God planned to send a Messiah to rescue sinners. Jesus is the promised Messiah. When they saw Him, **Simeon and Anna worshiped Jesus as the Messiah.**

- Bibles, 1 per kid
- Story Point Poster
- Small Group Timeline and Map Set (005802970)

Discussion & Bible skills (10 minutes)

Distribute Bibles. Guide boys and girls to open their Bibles

Older Kids Leader Guide
Unit 19 • Session 4

to Luke 2. Ask kids to name the four Gospels. (*Matthew, Mark, Luke, John*) Explain that when Mary and Joseph dedicated Jesus, they took Him to the temple in Jerusalem. [*Point out Jerusalem (H4) on the New Testament Israel Map.*] Choose a volunteer to read aloud Luke 2:30-32.

SAY • The Holy Spirit had led Simeon to the temple. Simeon saw Jesus and praised God because he recognized that God was going to use Jesus in His plan to bring salvation to the world. Anna also thanked God for the baby Jesus. **Simeon and Anna worshiped Jesus as the Messiah.**

Ask the following questions. Lead the group to discuss:

Option: Retell or review the Bible story using the bolded text of the Bible story script.

1. Why did Mary and Joseph dedicate Jesus? Why do some parents dedicate their children today? *Guide kids to recall that Mary and Joseph wanted to obey God's law by dedicating their Son. Sometimes parents today dedicate their children as a way to recognize that children belong to the Lord. If your church hosts dedication services for families, discuss the details: what dedication means and how everyone in the church commits to helping children know, love, and serve God.* (Option: Choose a kid to read 1 Kings 8:60-61.)

2. What does a life lived for God look like? How should the life of someone who trusts in Jesus as Lord and Savior differ from the life of someone who doesn't? *Lead kids to identify that the life of a believer should be marked by the work of the Holy Spirit in that person's life. The Holy Spirit grows us to become more like Christ. A believer recognizes Jesus as King and repents of sin. Differences are not always obvious, but unbelievers lack the Holy Spirit and are unrepentant.* (Option: Choose a volunteer to read Gal. 5:22-23.)

3. Why can we have peace even in difficult circumstances? *Encourage kids to discuss three types of peace—peace with God, peace that comes from God, and peace with others. We have a right relationship with God and look forward to a future with Him forever. Through the Spirit, God can give us peace in hard times.* (Option: Choose a volunteer to read Ps. 4:8.)

Activity choice (10 minutes)

OPTION 1: Travel bag sort

- "Missionaries Who Travel" printable
- luggage, 3 pieces of various sizes

Print and cut apart the "Missionaries Who Travel" printable. Place each missionary description in a piece of luggage that corresponds to the length of travel described: place the description of a volunteer missionary in the smallest bag, the description of a short-term missionary in the medium bag, and the description of the career missionary in the largest bag. Position the three pieces of luggage in different parts of the room.

Tip: Use this activity option to reinforce the missions moment from Teach the Story.

Walk around the room as a group, stopping at each bag. Ask a volunteer to open the bag and find the paper. Ask for a second volunteer to read the description.

SAY • One day, God may ask you to travel to another place to be a missionary. Maybe you will go for just a few days. Maybe you will spend a summer in another country. Or maybe you will move with your family to a new home where you will tell people about Jesus. No matter what God asks you to do, you can be obedient and help others know and worship Jesus.

LOW PREP

- Allergy Alert
- balloons

OPTION 2: Popcorn praise

Invite kids to stand in a circle. Explain that kids will work together to tap inflated balloons into the air so they don't fall to the floor. Each time a kid taps a balloon, she should say something to complete this sentence: "God, I praise You because …"

Begin with one balloon. Gradually introduce additional balloons. Continue as time allows.

SAY • When Simeon and Anna saw Jesus, they praised God. **Simeon and Anna worshiped Jesus as the Messiah.** We can praise God and worship Jesus as the Messiah. God has provided salvation through His Son, Jesus, for everyone who trusts in Him.

Option: Review the gospel with boys and girls. Explain that kids are welcome to speak with you or another teacher if they have questions.

Journal and prayer (5 minutes)

Distribute journal pages and pencils. Guide kids to think about and answer the questions listed on the page:

- What does this story teach me about God or the gospel?
- What does the story teach me about myself?
- Are there any commands in this story to obey? How are they for God's glory and my good?
- Are there any promises in this story to remember? How do they help me trust and love God?
- How does this story help me to live on mission better?

· pencils
· Journal Page
· "Who Did What?" activity page, 1 per kid

As kids journal, invite them to share their ideas. Then pray, thanking God for giving us His Word—the Bible—so we can learn about and know Jesus, the One who saves people from sin.

As time allows, lead kids to complete "Who Did What?" on the activity page. Kids should match each person from the Bible story to the correct description.

Tip: Give parents this week's *Big Picture Cards for Families* to allow families to interact with the biblical content at home.

Unit 19 · Session 5
Jesus as a Child

BIBLE PASSAGE:
Matthew 2; Luke 2

STORY POINT:
Even as a child, Jesus wanted to do His Father's plan.

KEY PASSAGE:
John 1:1-2

BIG PICTURE QUESTION:
Is Jesus God or a human?
As the Son of God, Jesus is both fully God and fully human.

INTRODUCE THE STORY	TEACH THE STORY	APPLY THE STORY
(10–15 MINUTES)	(25–30 MINUTES)	(25–30 MINUTES)
PAGE 70	PAGE 72	PAGE 78

 → →

Additional resources are available at gospelproject.com. For free training and session-by-session help, visit ministrygrid.com/gospelproject.

LEADER Bible Study

The Gospel of Luke records just two narratives about Jesus' childhood: His dedication (Luke 2:21-40) and His visit to the temple when He was 12 years old (Luke 2:41-52). The Gospel of Matthew includes another story: a visit from some wise men. These stories of Jesus as a child set the stage for Jesus' ministry as an adult.

After Jesus was born, God put a star in the sky as a sign. Wise men from the east followed the star to Jerusalem, looking for a new king. They found Jesus, who was probably 1 or 2 years old, in Bethlehem and they worshiped Him as King. Later, Jesus and His family settled in Nazareth, where Jesus grew up.

In Bible times, a Jewish boy became a man at 13. His father would train him to take on all the responsibilities of adulthood—social and spiritual. Joseph was a carpenter, and he likely trained Jesus in his trade. When Mary and Joseph went to Jerusalem to celebrate Passover, Joseph might have taken Jesus, who was about 12, around the city to teach Him the significance of the temple and to explain the purpose of the Passover feast.

Jesus' parents headed home after the feast. They assumed Jesus was among their traveling companions, but He wasn't. Jesus had stayed behind at the temple. A full day passed before Mary and Joseph noticed Jesus was missing. They hurried back to Jerusalem and finally found Him at the temple. Jesus asked His mother, "Didn't you know that I had to be in My Father's house?" Mary and Joseph did not understand. But Jesus is God's Son, and it was necessary that He honor His true Father. In all this, Jesus did not sin.

The Bible does not give many details about Jesus' childhood, but we know that as Jesus got older, He grew "in wisdom and stature, and in favor with God and with people" (Luke 2:52). Jesus carried out God's plan to reconcile the world to Himself. (2 Cor. 5:19)

5

The **BIBLE** Story

Jesus as a Child
Matthew 2; Luke 2

After Jesus was born, wise men followed a star to Bethlehem to find the new king of the Jews. The wise men worshiped Jesus as King. When they left, an angel told Joseph in a dream to leave Bethlehem because King Herod wanted to kill Jesus. So **Mary, Joseph, and Jesus** went to Egypt until Herod died. Then they **went back to** Israel and lived in **Nazareth. Jesus grew up in Nazareth.**

Every year, Jesus' parents traveled to Jerusalem for the Passover feast. Passover was the biggest holiday for the Jewish people. Many people traveled to Jerusalem to celebrate and remember when God saved His people from slavery in Egypt.

When Jesus was 12 years old, Jesus and His family went to Jerusalem together. When it was time to go home, Mary and Joseph began traveling to Nazareth with a large group of people. They didn't notice that Jesus was not with them; they thought He was among the group of travelers. But Jesus was not with the group. He had stayed behind in Jerusalem.

Mary and Joseph had been walking for a whole day when they started to look for Jesus. They looked among their relatives and friends, but they could not find Him. So Mary and Joseph **went back to Jerusalem. They searched everywhere for Jesus.** The city was so big, and Jesus was just a boy.

Finally, they found Him at the temple. Jesus was listening to the teachers and asking them questions. Everyone who heard Jesus could hardly believe how much Jesus understood. When Jesus' parents saw Him, they were surprised. Mary said, "Son, why have You done this? Your father and I were worried. We've been looking everywhere for You."

"Why were you looking for Me?" Jesus asked. "Didn't you know that I had to be in My Father's house?" But Mary and Joseph did not understand what Jesus was talking about. **Then Jesus went back to Nazareth with Mary and Joseph. Jesus was always obedient to them,** and Mary remembered all of these things.

As Jesus grew up, He became even wiser. God was pleased with Him, and so was everyone who knew Him.

Christ Connection: God sent Jesus to earth with a purpose. Even as a child, Jesus wanted to honor God. God blessed Jesus as He got ready to follow His Father's plan: to die on the cross and rescue people from sin.

Bible Storytelling Tips

- **Change positions:** Move around the room as you describe Mary and Joseph's journey.
- **Use facial expressions:** Reflect emotions of the story when Jesus was missing and when He was found.

INTRODUCE the Story

SESSION TITLE: Jesus as a Child
BIBLE PASSAGE: Matthew 2; Luke 2
STORY POINT: Even as a child, Jesus wanted to do His Father's plan.
KEY PASSAGE: John 1:1-2
BIG PICTURE QUESTION: Is Jesus God or a human? As the Son of God, Jesus
is both fully God and fully human.

Welcome time

Greet each kid as he or she arrives. Use this time to collect
the offering, fill out attendance sheets, and help new kids
connect to your group. Prompt kids to share about places
they like to travel with their families. Are there any places
they visit every year?

Activity page (5 minutes)

- "List of Learning"
  activity page,
  1 per kid
- pencils or markers

Invite kids to complete "List of Learning" on the activity
page. Guide kids to list things they have learned how to do
so far. (*how to walk, how to read*) Then encourage them to
list things they might learn in the future. (*how to drive*)

SAY • Are you surprised by some of the things you can do
even as a kid? You'll learn much more as you grow.
Did you know God can use you in His kingdom?
Today's Bible story gives us a picture of what Jesus
was like when He was just 12 years old.

LOW PREP

- chalkboard or dry
  erase board
- chalk or markers
- eraser

Session starter (10 minutes)

OPTION 1: Amazing feats
Explain that several world records are held by kids who have
accomplished amazing feats. Form two teams. Describe a

world record and ask a question. Team members should agree on a guess and write it on the board. Award one point to the team closest to the correct answer.

- A 9-year-old boy set the world record for most claps in 1 minute. How many times did he clap? (*1,080*)
- A team of 12 jumpers and 2 rope holders set the world record for most jumps over a rope in 1 minute. How many times did they jump? (*230*)
- A fifth grade girl set the record for longest distance to stretch homemade slime in 30 seconds. How many inches did it stretch? (*88*)
- A 17-year-old boy set the record for the world's largest drawing. How many square feet did it cover? (*3,486*)
- A group of children set the record for largest gathering of people dressed as rabbits. How many children participated? (*1,119*)

SAY • Those were some amazing feats! Did you know that when Jesus was 12 years old, teachers in the temple were amazed by Him?

OPTION 2: Seek and find

Before the session, hide people figures around the room. Challenge kids to find the figures. If time allows, choose volunteers to hide the figures again while the rest of the group faces a wall and closes their eyes. Then play again.

· miniature people figures

SAY • Finding those people in the room wasn't easy. Imagine looking for one person in a city of thousands of people! That's what Mary and Joseph had to do in today's Bible story.

Transition to teach the story

Into the World

TEACH the Story

SESSION TITLE: Jesus as a Child
BIBLE PASSAGE: Matthew 2; Luke 2
STORY POINT: Even as a child, Jesus wanted to do His Father's plan.
KEY PASSAGE: John 1:1-2
BIG PICTURE QUESTION: Is Jesus God or a human? As the Son of God, Jesu
is both fully God and fully human.

Countdown

· countdown video

Show the countdown video as you transition to teach the story. Set it to end as the session begins.

Introduce the session (3 minutes)

· leader attire
· camera
· backpack
· Bible
· school yearbook

Tip: If you prefer not to use themed content or characters, adapt or omit this introduction.

[Leader enters carrying a camera and a backpack. The backpack contains a Bible and a school yearbook.]

LEADER • Hi, everyone! I am so glad you're here. I'm [*your name*], a studio photographer. Have you ever gotten your picture taken at school for the yearbook? Do you like picture day? When I was a kid, picture day always made me nervous. I had to decide what I was going to wear and how to fix my hair. My mom saved my school picture every year and put them all in a frame so she could see how I grew over the years [*Retrieve a yearbook.*] Sometimes schools hire me to take yearbook photos and I do my best to make kids feel comfortable. As a kid, you're changing so much! It's fun to be able to look back at pictures of when you were younger and see how you've grown.

[*Retrieve a Bible.*] I'm excited to share today's Bible story with you. It's about a Jesus' time as a child. The

Bible doesn't tell us a lot about Jesus before He was around 30 years old, but two particular events are recorded in the Scriptures. Let's find out more.

Big picture question (1 minute)

LEADER • First, does anyone remember our big picture question and answer? [*Allow kids to respond.*] ***Is Jesus God or a human? As the Son of God, Jesus is both fully God and fully human.*** This can be kind of hard to wrap your mind around, but it's important to realize that when God the Son came to earth, He did not give up being God. He took on the likeness of humanity [*see Phil. 2:7*] and experienced life like we do, as fully human, to perfectly obey the Father and to rescue sinners.

Giant timeline (1 minute)

Show the giant timeline. Point to individual Bible stories as you review.

• Giant Timeline

LEADER • In today's Bible story, we'll hear about Jesus as a small child and also as a 12-year-old. Let's review what we've learned about Jesus so far. First, we learned about Jesus' family. **Jesus' family line proved He is the Messiah.** Before Jesus came into the world, John was born. God had plan for John's life. **John was born to prepare the way for Jesus.** Then, at just the right time, Jesus was born. Why was Jesus born? **Jesus was born to be God's promised Savior.**

When Jesus was about five weeks old, His earthly parents—Mary and Joseph—took Him to the temple to be dedicated. At the temple, **Simeon and Anna worshiped Jesus as the Messiah.** So what happened between the time Jesus was dedicated and the time He was a grown man? Listen to today's Bible story: "Jesus as a Child."

Tell the Bible story (10 minutes)

- Bibles
- "Jesus as a Child" video
- Big Picture Question Poster
- Bible Story Picture Poster
- Story Point Poster

Open your Bible to Luke 2. Use the Bible storytelling tips on the Bible story page to help you tell the story, or show the Bible story video "Jesus as a Child."

LEADER • At the beginning of the story, we heard about the wise men visiting Jesus. Jesus might have been one or two years old when they came. He and His parents were still in Bethlehem. But they later moved to Nazareth, and that's where Jesus grew up. The next story the Bible records about Jesus is about 10 years later, when Jesus was 12 years old. Do you remember where they went? (*Jerusalem*) Why did they go? (*to celebrate Passover*)

When the feast was over, Mary and Joseph started traveling home. But Jesus stayed behind. How do you think Mary and Joseph felt when they realized Jesus was missing? They hurried back to Jerusalem and searched the city. When Mary and Joseph found Jesus, He was in the temple with the Jewish teachers. What did the teachers in the temple think about Jesus? Look at Luke 2:47. [*Allow kids to read the verse and respond.*] They were astonished at His understanding.

What did Jesus call the temple? Look at Luke 2:29. [*Allow kids to read the verse and respond.*] Jesus called the temple His Father's house. **Even as a child, Jesus wanted to do His Father's plan.** The Gospel of Luke says one more thing about Jesus as a child: As Jesus grew up, He became wiser and increased in favor with God and people. [*See Luke 2:52.*]

Christ connection

LEADER • God sent Jesus to earth with a purpose. Even as a child, Jesus wanted to honor God. God blessed Jesus as He got ready to follow His Father's plan: to die on the cross and rescue people from sin.

Tip: Use Scripture and the guide provided on page 77 to explain how to become a Christian. Make sure kids know when and where they can ask questions.

Questions from kids video (3 minutes)

Show the "Unit 19, Session 5" questions from kids video. Prompt kids to think about how they feel about sharing the gospel with others. Guide them to discuss ways they can share their testimony with confidence.

· "Unit 19, Session 5" questions from kids video

Missions moment (3 minutes)

Display the photos from Brazil and ask a volunteer to read each caption. Ask the kids what they think it means for Christians to follow God's plan on mission in Brazil, or anywhere we go. Allow time for kids to discuss.

· "Photos from Brazil" printable

LEADER • **Even as a child, Jesus wanted to do His Father's plan.** Even though you are young, you can follow God's plan and be on mission wherever you go!

Key passage (5 minutes)

Show the key passage poster. Lead the boys and girls to read together John 1:1-2.

· Key Passage Poster
· "The Word Was God (John 1:1-2)" song

LEADER • Memorizing God's Word helps us remember what is true about God and about ourselves. Our key passage tells us that God the Son is the Word. He has always existed, and everything was created through Him. He is God, and we are not. Let's sing our key passage song together.

Lead kids in singing "The Word Was God (John 1:1-2)."

Sing (4 minutes)

- "Take It to the Lord"
  song
- Bible

Open your Bible and read aloud 2 Corinthians 4:6.

LEADER • When God sent Jesus into the world, He sent
light into darkness. When we know Jesus, we see
God's glory and greatness. ***Is Jesus God or a human?
As the Son of God, Jesus is both fully God and fully
human.*** He is worthy of praise. Let's sing.

Sing together "Take It to the Lord."

Pray (2 minutes)

Invite kids to pray before dismissing to apply the story.

LEADER • Lord God, thank You for Your Word. We want
to honor You. Help us to trust You and follow Your
plan. Give us wisdom. Thank You that our future is
secure because of Jesus. We love You. Amen.

Dismiss to apply the story

The Gospel: God's Plan for Me

Ask kids if they have ever heard the word *gospel*. Clarify that the word *gospel* means "good news." It is the message about Christ, the kingdom of God, and salvation. Use the following guide to share the gospel with kids.

God rules. Explain to kids that the Bible tells us God created everything, and He is in charge of everything. Invite a volunteer to read Genesis 1:1 from the Bible. Read Revelation 4:11 or Colossians 1:16-17 aloud and explain what these verses mean.

We sinned. Tell kids that since the time of Adam and Eve, everyone has chosen to disobey God. (Romans 3:23) The Bible calls this sin. Because God is holy, God cannot be around sin. Sin separates us from God and deserves God's punishment of death. (Romans 6:23)

God provided. Choose a child to read John 3:16 aloud. Say that God sent His Son, Jesus, the perfect solution to our sin problem, to rescue us from the punishment we deserve. It's something we, as sinners, could never earn on our own. Jesus alone saves us. Read and explain Ephesians 2:8-9.

Jesus gives. Share with kids that Jesus lived a perfect life, died on the cross for our sins, and rose again. Because Jesus gave up His life for us, we can be welcomed into God's family for eternity. This is the best gift ever! Read Romans 5:8; 2 Corinthians 5:21; or 1 Peter 3:18.

We respond. Tell kids that they can respond to Jesus. Read Romans 10:9-10,13. Review these aspects of our response: Believe in your heart that Jesus alone saves you through what He's already done on the cross. Repent, turning from self and sin to Jesus. Tell God and others that your faith is in Jesus.

Offer to talk with any child who is interested in responding to Jesus. Provide *I'm a Christian Now!* for new Christians to take home and complete with their families.

APPLY the Story

SESSION TITLE: Jesus as a Child

BIBLE PASSAGE: Matthew 2; Luke 2

STORY POINT: Even as a child, Jesus wanted to do His Father's plan.

KEY PASSAGE: John 1:1-2

BIG PICTURE QUESTION: Is Jesus God or a human? As the Son of God, Jesus is both fully God and fully human.

Key passage activity (5 minutes)

· Key Passage Poster

Instruct boys and girls to stand in a circle. Display the key passage poster. Lead kids in reading John 1:1-2 aloud together. Assign each kid a number: *1, 2* or *3*. Explain that kids will say the key passage together. When kids say "beginning," the 1s will clap. When kids say "Word," the 2s will clap. When kids say "God," the 3s will clap. Repeat as time allows.

SAY • In his Gospel, John answered the question, who is Jesus? We know that Jesus is God the Son. We know that Jesus came to earth. **Even as a child, Jesus wanted to do His Father's plan.** So *is Jesus God or a human?* Let's say our big picture answer together: *As the Son of God, Jesus is both fully God and fully human.*

Discussion & Bible skills (10 minutes)

· Bibles, 1 per kid
· Story Point Poster
· Small Group Timeline and Map Set (005802970)

Distribute Bibles. Guide boys and girls to open their Bibles to Luke 2. Ask kids to recall what the Gospel—Matthew, Mark, Luke, and John—are about. (*Jesus' life, death, and resurrection*)

SAY • We don't know a lot about Jesus' time as a child.

The Gospels tell us that wise men followed a star to Bethlehem and worshiped Jesus when He was a small boy. [*Point to Bethlehem (I4) on the New Testament Israel Map.*] He grew up in Nazareth with His earthly parents, Mary and Joseph. [*Point to Nazareth (E5).*] When Jesus was about 12 years old, He went with Mary and Joseph to celebrate Passover in Jerusalem. [*Point to Jerusalem (H4).*] In today's Bible story, we see that **even as a child, Jesus wanted to do His Father's plan.**

Option: Retell or review the Bible story using the bolded text of the Bible story script.

Choose a volunteer to read aloud Luke 2:51-52. Then ask the following questions. Lead the group to discuss:

1. Who does God want us to honor and why? *Help kids connect from the story that like Jesus, we should seek to honor God. God commands us to honor our parents. We should also honor other believers. The Bible says we should outdo one another in showing honor.*
   (Option: Choose a volunteer to read Rom. 12:10.)

2. How can we grow in wisdom and obedience to God? *Invite kids to share their ideas. Emphasize that we grow through the power of the Holy Spirit. Encourage kids to read the Bible consistently, pray, and spend time in fellowship with other believers.*
   (Option: Choose a volunteer to read Heb. 10:24-25.)

3. How can God use you in His kingdom even while you are young? *Invite kids to share ideas of ways they can serve God when they are young. Emphasize that God can use anyone who is willing to obey Him. God's plan for us is better than any plan we can imagine for ourselves. We can rely on the Holy Spirit to lead us as we follow Jesus.*
   (Option: Choose a volunteer to read Eph. 1:9-10.)

Activity choice (10 minutes)

Tip: Use this activity option to reinforce the missions moment from Teach the Story.

 OPTION 1: Service project

Involve your kids in a simple service project in the church. Here are some ideas: sort cans in the food pantry, clean toys in the nursery, pick up trash around the church building, sweep the hallways, or clean up the kitchen. Consider asking your church staff about a simple task for kids to complete.

SAY • You are a part of God's plan right now. You are also an important part of this church. Everyone in the church can be a part of God's mission by doing things that serve others. Let's spend a few minutes doing a project in the church that serves others. Our mission as a church is to lead others to Jesus; so when we serve at church, we are a part of the mission.

LOW PREP

·Bibles
·chair

OPTION 2: Hot seat

Assign three volunteers the following roles: Mary, Joseph, and Jesus. Choose one role player to sit at the front of the room. Invite kids to interview the player, asking questions about the Bible story as if they are conducting an investigation.

Suggest kids ask "who, what, when, where, and how" questions. The player should respond as that person. Provide Bibles and allow players to refer to Luke 2:39-52.

Players may be creative with their answers, but strive for biblical accuracy. After several questions, select another role player to take the "hot seat."

SAY • I wonder if Mary and Joseph asked Jesus more questions as they traveled home together. Remember our big picture question: *Is Jesus God or a human? As the Son of God, Jesus is both fully God and fully*

human. God sent Jesus to earth with a purpose. **Even as a child, Jesus wanted to do His Father's plan.** God blessed Jesus as He got ready to follow His Father's plan: to die on the cross and rescue people from sin.

When we trust in Jesus as Lord and Savior, God forgives our sin and gives us eternal life.

Option: Review the gospel with boys and girls. Explain that kids are welcome to speak with you or another teacher if they have questions.

Journal and prayer (5 minutes)

Distribute journal pages and pencils. Guide kids to think about and answer the questions listed on the page:

- What does this story teach me about God or the gospel?
- What does the story teach me about myself?
- Are there any commands in this story to obey? How are they for God's glory and my good?
- Are there any promises in this story to remember? How do they help me trust and love God?
- How does this story help me to live on mission better?

· pencils
· Journal Page
· "Lost and Found" activity page, 1 per kid

As kids journal, invite them to share their ideas. Then pray, thanking God for His Word and for sending His Son. Ask Him to show grace to kids as they grow in wisdom and understanding.

As time allows, lead kids to complete "Lost and Found" on the activity page. Kids should help Mary and Joseph find their way back to Jesus by following the path containing the words of today's Bible story point.

Tip: Give parents this week's *Big Picture Cards for Families* to allow families to interact with the biblical content at home.

Unit 20 · Session 1
Jesus' Baptism

BIBLE PASSAGE:
Matthew 3; Mark 1; Luke 3; John 1

STORY POINT:
Jesus obeyed God by being baptized.

KEY PASSAGE:
John 3:30

BIG PICTURE QUESTION:
Why did Jesus become human? Jesus became human to obey His Father's plan and rescue sinners.

INTRODUCE THE STORY (10–15 MINUTES) PAGE 86	TEACH THE STORY (25–30 MINUTES) PAGE 88	APPLY THE STORY (25–30 MINUTES) PAGE 94
	→ 	→ 

Additional resources are available at gospelproject.com. For free training and session-by-session help, visit ministrygrid.com/gospelproject.

LEADER Bible Study

Zechariah's son, John, grew up in the wilderness. His ministry began when God's word came to him, and he began preaching near the Jordan River. John worked to get people ready for the coming of Jesus, fulfilling the Old Testament prophecy, "A voice of one crying out: Prepare the way of the LORD in the wilderness" (Isa. 40:3a).

John called people to repent of their sins, and he baptized them in the Jordan River. John also instructed people on right living. (See Luke 3:10-14.) Some of the people suspected that John might be the Messiah, but John insisted, "One who is more powerful than I am is coming" (Luke 3:16).

Before His ministry began, Jesus came from Galilee to be baptized by John at the Jordan River. But John was calling people to a baptism of repentance. Jesus never sinned (see Heb. 4:15; 2 Cor. 5:21), so why did Jesus come to be baptized? John recognized this when he said, "I need to be baptized by you, and yet you come to me?" (Matt. 3:14).

Commentators' ideas vary about why exactly Jesus was baptized. Perhaps He was affirming John's work. Maybe He was identifying with sinners or showing them how they would be saved—through His death, burial, and resurrection. Jesus answered John, "Allow it for now, because this is the way for us to fulfill all righteousness" (Matt. 3:15). Jesus completely obeyed God, and God audibly confirmed His sonship.

As you teach, allow time for kids to ask questions about repentance, salvation, and baptism. Emphasize that baptism is not what saves us; baptism is a way we show that we have been saved. Baptism reminds us that when we trust in Jesus, we die to sin and come into a new way of life—a life lived for Him. (See Rom. 6:3-4.)

The **BIBLE** Story

Jesus' Baptism
Matthew 3; Mark 1; Luke 3; John 1

John the Baptist lived in the wilderness. His clothes were made out of camel's hair and he wore a leather belt around his waist. He ate locusts and wild honey. **John began telling people, "Repent and be baptized because God's kingdom is almost here."**

Some people asked John, "Who are you?" John said, "I am not the Messiah." John also said he wasn't Elijah, and he wasn't the Prophet that God had promised to send after Moses.

"Who are you, then?" they asked.

Long before John was born, the prophet Isaiah said, "Someone is shouting in the wilderness. He says, 'Prepare the way for the Lord; make His paths straight!'" Isaiah was talking about John. John had a very important job. He **was supposed to get people ready for Jesus—God's promised Messiah. People started to repent; they turned away from their sins and turned to God for forgiveness. Then John baptized them in the Jordan River.** Baptism was a picture that the people's sins had been washed away.

John preached, "Someone greater than me is coming. I am not worthy to remove His sandals. **I baptize you with water, but He will**

baptize you with the Holy Spirit."

By this time, Jesus was an adult. He went to see John the Baptist at the Jordan River. When John saw Jesus, he said, "Here is the Lamb of God, who takes away the sin of the world!"

Jesus told John that He wanted to be baptized. But John didn't think he should baptize Jesus. "I need You to baptize me," John said. "Why do You want me to baptize You?" John was confused. He baptized people who confessed their sins; Jesus never sinned!

Jesus said, "Allow Me to be baptized. God says this is right." So John agreed, and he baptized Jesus.

Jesus immediately came up out of the water. Suddenly, the heavens opened and Jesus saw the Holy Spirit coming down on Him like a dove. God's voice came from heaven. "This is My Son," the voice said. "I love Him, and I am very pleased with Him!"

Christ Connection: Jesus never sinned, but He obeyed God and was baptized like sinners are baptized. Baptism reminds us of Jesus' death and resurrection. It reminds us that when we trust in Jesus, we turn from sin and start a new life—a life lived for Jesus.

Bible Storytelling Tips

- **Use gestures:** Hold up your arms when speaking John's dialogue.
- **Display art:** Show the Bible story picture and point to elements of the scene at appropriate points in the story.

INTRODUCE the Story

SESSION TITLE: Jesus' Baptism
BIBLE PASSAGE: Matthew 3; Mark 1; Luke 3; John 1
STORY POINT: Jesus obeyed God by being baptized.
KEY PASSAGE: John 3:30
BIG PICTURE QUESTION: Why did Jesus become human? Jesus became human to obey His Father's plan and rescue sinners.

Welcome time

Greet each kid as he or she arrives. Use this time to collect the offering, fill out attendance sheets, and help new kids connect to your group. Prompt kids to share things kids can do that would be pleasing to parents.

Activity page (5 minutes)

· "Baptism Words" activity page, 1 per kid
· pencils or markers

Invite kids to complete "Baptism Words" on the activity page. Challenge kids to list as many words as they can think of that they can form using the letters in the word *BAPTISM*. Lead kids to share their lists.

SAY • Great job! The letters in the word baptism can be rearranged to spell words like *stamp, past, maps, sit, spa,* and so on. Can anyone tell me what *baptism* means? *[Allow kids to respond.]* Today we will learn more about what baptism is and who should be baptized.

Session starter (10 minutes)

OPTION 1: Special handshakes
Invite each kid to make a personalized special handshake with you. Suggest kids incorporate high-fives, fist bumps,

Older Kids Leader Guide
Unit 20 • Session 1

hand-clapping, and other moves. Practice each handshake a few times. Then lead kids to line up and demonstrate their handshake with you or their group members.

SAY • People all over the world shake hands as a greeting. It's a sign to say, "Hello, nice to meet you." What other actions do we do that communicate messages without using words? (*waving, bowing, hugging, saluting, crossing your arms*) What do they mean?

In the Bible story we will hear today, we'll learn about baptism—a symbol that shows what it means to follow Jesus.

Tip: If your group is large, form smaller groups and instruct the kids in each group to formulate a handshake to do with one another.

OPTION 2: Circle crossing

Instruct kids to stand or sit in a circle. Stand in the center and say, "Cross the circle if you … [*announce something you can do or have done*]." (Examples: if you have brown eyes, if you have ever danced in the rain, if you have bowled a strike, can bake a cake, and so on)

Players who can also do or who have also done that thing should cross the circle and sit in the seat of someone else who crossed the circle. End the game with these two prompts: if you have ever sinned, if you have ever been baptized or seen someone else be baptized.

SAY • In the Bible story we are going to hear today, Jesus was baptized like sinners are baptized. But Jesus never sinned! Listen closely to our story to find out why Jesus was baptized.

Transition to teach the story

TEACH the Story

SESSION TITLE: Jesus' Baptism
BIBLE PASSAGE: Matthew 3; Mark 1; Luke 3; John 1
STORY POINT: Jesus obeyed God by being baptized.
KEY PASSAGE: John 3:30
BIG PICTURE QUESTION: Why did Jesus become human? Jesus became human to obey His Father's plan and rescue sinners.

· room decorations
· Theme Background Slide (optional)

Suggested Theme Decorating Ideas: Simulate a road construction site by setting up traffic cones at the front of the room. Use markers and orange poster board to create traffic signs that say *ROAD CLOSED* or *WORK AREA AHEAD*. Position a wheelbarrow, push broom, and shovel at one side. Consider hanging black poster board as a traffic message board. Cut letters from yellow paper and change the message each session. You may also display the theme background slide.

Countdown

· countdown video

Show the countdown video as you transition to teach the story. Set it to end as the session begins.

Introduce the session (3 minutes)

· leader attire
· stop sign
· message board

Tip: If you prefer not to use themed content or characters, adapt or omit this introduction.

[Leader enters wearing khaki pants, a reflective shirt or vest, and a hard hat. Leader carries a stop sign made from poster board attached to a tall broomstick. A traffic message board reads HIGH WATER.]

LEADER • Hi, everyone! I'm *[your name]*. It's nice to meet you. I'm going to have to ask you not to approach the construction area. You see, some work crews have been repairing a bridge and for the last several days it has rained and rained. Now the water from the creek below is almost covering the road. So they hired me—a traffic control specialist—to stand here and make sure no one crosses behind the barriers. Did you know that many cars will float in just 12 inches of water? A couple of drivers have come by here insisting they can make it across the bridge safely, but I tell them, "Turn around; don't drown!"

As you might imagine, standing here all day can get kind of boring. So when there's no traffic, I've been telling myself stories that I remember reading in the Bible. Can I share a story with you?

Big picture question (1 minute)

LEADER • This story is about a couple of guys—John and Jesus—who went into a river. One of them even went under the water! But don't worry; this story has a happy ending. First, can any of you tell me who John was? And who is Jesus? [*Allow kids to respond.*] Jesus is God the Son. He came to earth as a human. As you hear today's story about Him, think about this big picture question: **Why did Jesus become human?** Listen carefully to the story to see if you can figure out the answer.

Giant timeline (1 minute)

Show the giant timeline. Point to individual Bible stories as you review.

· Giant Timeline

LEADER • Today's story comes near the beginning of the New Testament. Before this, the stories from the New Testament have been about Jesus' family line, the birth of John the Baptist, the birth of Jesus, and

Jesus' childhood. Today's story took place almost 20 years after Mary and Joseph found Jesus in the temple, which Jesus called "My Father's house" (Luke 2:49).

Tell the Bible story (10 minutes)

- Bibles
- "Jesus' Baptism" video
- Big Picture Question Poster
- Bible Story Picture Poster
- Story Point Poster

Open your Bible to Matthew 3; Mark 1; Luke 3; John 1. Use the Bible storytelling tips on the Bible story page to help you tell the story, or show the Bible story video "Jesus' Baptism."

LEADER • John's job was to get people ready for Jesus. He told people that Jesus was coming, and he told them to repent and be baptized. Can anyone tell me what it means to repent? (*to be sorry for your sin, to turn away from your sin, and to turn toward God*)

John baptized people in the Jordan River as a picture that their sins had been washed away. While John was baptizing people, Jesus came to the river. Jesus told John that He wanted to be baptized. John was confused. He had been baptizing people who confessed their sins. But Jesus never sinned. What did Jesus tell John next? Look at Matthew 3:15. [*Allow kids to read the verse and respond.*]

Jesus said it was the right thing to do, so John baptized Jesus. Jesus wasn't baptized as a sign of repentance but as a way of fully obeying the Father. **Jesus obeyed God by being baptized.** Let's say our big picture question and answer together: *Why did Jesus become human? Jesus became human to obey His Father's plan and rescue sinners.*

When Jesus came out of the water, the heavens opened and God's Spirit came down like a dove.

Think about the sound of water dripping off of Jesus' body. Then a voice came from heaven. What did the voice say? Look at Matthew 3:17. [*Allow kids to read the verse and respond.*]

Christ connection

LEADER • Jesus never sinned, but He obeyed God and was baptized like sinners are baptized. Baptism reminds us of Jesus' death and resurrection. Jesus died on the cross for our sin. After three days, God raised Him from the dead. Baptism reminds us of Jesus and what He did to save people from sin. When we trust in Jesus, we turn from sin and start a new life—a life lived for Jesus.

Tip: Use Scripture and the guide provided on page 93 to explain how to become a Christian. Make sure kids know when and where they can ask questions.

Questions from kids video (3 minutes)

Show the "Unit 20, Session 1" questions from kids video. Prompt kids to think about why people are baptized. Guide them to discuss a time they saw a baptism or share any questions they have about baptism.

· "Unit 20, Session 1" questions from kids video

 ## Missions moment (3 minutes)

LEADER • It's time to learn about an exciting missions organization called Mission Aviation Fellowship (MAF). Some villages are hard to reach by car and would take days to hike to on foot; however, missionary pilots can fly small airplanes into these villages. We know that **Jesus obeyed God by being baptized.** Many people have heard about Jesus, have trusted in Him, and were baptized because of the work of MAF.

Play the "Introduction to MAF" missions video. Then

· "Introduction to MAF" missions video

pray, thanking God for missionary pilots and their work in spreading the gospel.

Key passage (5 minutes)

· Key Passage Poster
· "He Must Increase, but I Must Decrease (John 3:30)" song

Show the key passage poster. Lead the boys and girls to read together John 3:30.

LEADER • John the Baptist spoke these words to His disciples when they asked him about Jesus. Many people thought John might be the Messiah. He had increased as people began to follow him. So John made it clear: Jesus was the One they were waiting for. John knew he had a role to play, and he could not distract people from the Lamb of God—Jesus, the promised Messiah.

Lead kids in singing "He Must Increase, but I Must Decrease (John 3:30)."

Sing (4 minutes)

· "Take It to the Lord" song
· Bible

Open your Bible and read aloud Psalm 99:2-3.

LEADER • When we trust in Jesus, we turn from sin and start a new life—a life lived for Jesus. He is great and exalted above all. Let's praise His name together.

Sing together "Take It to the Lord."

Pray (2 minutes)

Invite kids to pray before dismissing to apply the story.

LEADER • Lord God, we don't have to clean ourselves up before we come to You. Thank You for the blessing of baptism and the reminder of death to sin and new life in Christ. May You receive glory. Amen.

Dismiss to apply the story

The Gospel: God's Plan for Me

Ask kids if they have ever heard the word *gospel*. Clarify that the word *gospel* means "good news." It is the message about Christ, the kingdom of God, and salvation. Use the following guide to share the gospel with kids.

God rules. Explain to kids that the Bible tells us God created everything, and He is in charge of everything. Invite a volunteer to read Genesis 1:1 from the Bible. Read Revelation 4:11 or Colossians 1:16-17 aloud and explain what these verses mean.

We sinned. Tell kids that since the time of Adam and Eve, everyone has chosen to disobey God. (Romans 3:23) The Bible calls this sin. Because God is holy, God cannot be around sin. Sin separates us from God and deserves God's punishment of death. (Romans 6:23)

God provided. Choose a child to read John 3:16 aloud. Say that God sent His Son, Jesus, the perfect solution to our sin problem, to rescue us from the punishment we deserve. It's something we, as sinners, could never earn on our own. Jesus alone saves us. Read and explain Ephesians 2:8-9.

Jesus gives. Share with kids that Jesus lived a perfect life, died on the cross for our sins, and rose again. Because Jesus gave up His life for us, we can be welcomed into God's family for eternity. This is the best gift ever! Read Romans 5:8; 2 Corinthians 5:21; or 1 Peter 3:18.

We respond. Tell kids that they can respond to Jesus. Read Romans 10:9-10,13. Review these aspects of our response: Believe in your heart that Jesus alone saves you through what He's already done on the cross. Repent, turning from self and sin to Jesus. Tell God and others that your faith is in Jesus.

Offer to talk with any child who is interested in responding to Jesus. Provide *I'm a Christian Now!* for new Christians to take home and complete with their families.

APPLY the Story

SESSION TITLE: Jesus' Baptism
BIBLE PASSAGE: Matthew 3; Mark 1; Luke 3; John 1
STORY POINT: Jesus obeyed God by being baptized.
KEY PASSAGE: John 3:30
BIG PICTURE QUESTION: Why did Jesus become human? Jesus became human to obey His Father's plan and rescue sinners.

Key passage activity (5 minutes)

- Key Passage Poster
- dry erase board or large sheet of paper
- marker
- eraser

Display the key passage poster. Lead kids in reading aloud John 3:30. Then write the key passage on a dry erase board, leaving blanks for several of the words. Challenge kids to fill in the blanks. Play again with more blanks, working up to kids filling in all the words from memory.

SAY • In today's Bible story, **Jesus obeyed God by being baptized.** John baptized Jesus in the Jordan River. Later, when John's followers asked John the Baptist about Jesus, John said these words to his disciples.

This is the same attitude we should have about Jesus, that He should increase and we should decrease. Work on memorizing this verse during the week.

Discussion & Bible skills (10 minutes)

- Bibles, 1 per kid
- Story Point Poster
- Small Group Timeline and Map Set (005802970)

Distribute Bibles. Guide boys and girls to open their Bibles to Matthew 3. Explain that the Book of Matthew was written to show that Jesus is the Messiah God promised. Choose a volunteer to read aloud Matthew 3:16-17.

SAY • **Jesus obeyed God by being baptized.** Jesus' obedience pleased God. When we obey God in faith, our obedience pleases Him too. One way we can respond to God in obedience is by being baptized. Ask the following questions. Lead the group to discuss:

Option: Retell or review the Bible story using the bolded text of the Bible story script.

1. What message do we declare when we are baptized? *Emphasize that when someone is baptized, that person follows Jesus' example by showing others that he or she has confessed Jesus as Savior and Lord. Lead kids to connect going under the water in baptism as dying to sin and coming up from the water as being raised to new life—a life lived for Jesus. Point out that Jesus' baptism symbolized what would come: His death, burial, and resurrection.*
   (Option: Choose a volunteer to read Rom. 6:4.)

2. Where do we see the Trinity—the three Persons of God—in today's Bible story? *Help kids recognize God the Father speaking from heaven, God the Son on earth as a man, and God the Spirit appearing like a dove. Emphasize that there is one God, and He exists as the Father, Son, and Holy Spirit. Acknowledge that the Trinity can be hard to understand; no one is like God!*
   (Option: Choose a volunteer to read Eph. 2:18.)

3. Why does obedience to God bring Him glory? *Lead kids to share their ideas. Prompt them to think about how obeying God shows that we trust Him and submit to Him as Lord of our lives. In a similar way, God is glorified when we live like Jesus—loving God and loving others, obeying His commands, and remaining in Him.*
   (Option: Choose a kid to read 1 John 3:23-24.)

- "Welcome to MAF"
  printable
- crayons

Tip: Use this
activity option
to reinforce the
missions moment
from Teach the
Story.

Activity choice (10 minutes)

OPTION 1: Learn about MAF

Give each kid a "Welcome to MAF" activity sheet. Ask a volunteer to read the story at the top of the page aloud. Help kids unscramble the words (*airplanes, world, love, people, villages*). Then ask another volunteer to read the coded message aloud.

SAY • The missionary pilots and the other MAF workers are able to share Jesus' love with people whom no one can reach! They can deliver food and medical supplies, transport people to hospitals, and most importantly, they can teach people about Jesus.

Because we have died with Christ and have been raised to new life through Him, we call on others to repent of their sin, trust in Christ, and be baptized.

Note: Consider asking parents or church members to donate travel-size toiletry items for a mission project included in session 3 of this unit.

- "Origami Dove
  Instructions"
  printable
- construction paper or
  origami paper
- scissors
- markers

OPTION 2: Origami dove

Before the session, use the instructions to form an origami dove as a sample.

Print a copy of the origami dove instructions for each kid. Provide origami paper or cut construction paper into 4- to 6-inch squares. Lead kids in following the origami instructions step by step. Encourage them to draw eyes on the dove when they finish.

SAY • What part did a dove play in today's Bible story? [*Allow kids to respond.*] **Jesus obeyed God by being baptized.** When Jesus came out of the water, the heavens opened and Jesus saw the Holy Spirit coming down on Him like a dove. God's voice came from heaven: "This is My Son. I love Him, and I am very pleased with Him!" Say our big picture question and answer with me: *Why did Jesus become human? Jesus became human to obey His Father's plan and rescue sinners.*

Option: Review the gospel with boys and girls. Explain that kids are welcome to speak with you or another teacher if they have questions.

Journal and prayer (5 minutes)

Distribute journal pages and pencils. Guide kids to think about and answer the questions listed on the page:

- What does this story teach me about God or the gospel?
- What does the story teach me about myself?
- Are there any commands in this story to obey? How are they for God's glory and my good?
- Are there any promises in this story to remember? How do they help me trust and love God?
- How does this story help me to live on mission better?

- pencils
- Journal Page
- "Tell the Story" activity page, 1 per kid

As kids journal, invite them to share their ideas. Then pray, thanking God for His Word and for Jesus' example of obedience through baptism. Pray that kids would trust in Jesus and follow His example in baptism. Thank Him for new life in Christ.

As time allows, lead kids to complete "Tell the Story" on the activity page. Kids should find and read the Scripture references in their Bibles and then write out in their own words what happened in the Bible story.

Tip: Give parents this week's *Big Picture Cards for Families* to allow families to interact with the biblical content at home.

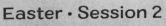
Use Week of:

Easter • Session 2
Jesus' Crucifixion and Resurrection

BIBLE PASSAGE:
Matthew 26–28; 1 Corinthians 15

STORY POINT:
Jesus' resurrection gives us hope for eternal life.

KEY PASSAGE:
John 3:30

BIG PICTURE QUESTION:
Why did Jesus become human? Jesus became human to obey His Father's plan and rescue sinners.

INTRODUCE THE STORY	TEACH THE STORY	APPLY THE STORY
(10–15 MINUTES)	(25–30 MINUTES)	(25–30 MINUTES)
PAGE 102	**PAGE 104**	**PAGE 110**

 → →

Additional resources are available at gospelproject.com. For free training and session-by-session help, visit ministrygrid.com/gospelproject.

LEADER Bible Study

Jesus' crucifixion and resurrection are essential to the Christian faith. If we teach Jesus as a respected teacher and miracle-worker who claimed to be the Messiah and who was crucified on the cross—but who was not resurrected—then we are teaching the Jesus of Judaism. If we teach Jesus as a wise teacher and prophet who ascended into heaven—but who was not crucified—then we are teaching the Jesus of Islam.

Jesus' purpose for coming to earth was to save us from our sins. (Matt. 1:21) Jesus came to die to show God's love to us (Rom. 5:7-8) so that whoever believes in Him will not perish but have eternal life. (John 3:16) Jesus came to die so that we would be forgiven. (Eph. 1:7) Jesus came to die to bring us to God. (1 Pet. 3:18)

Jesus died on the cross to satisfy the wrath of God toward sin. His resurrection proved that God was satisfied with Jesus' sacrifice. If Jesus had died but not been raised up, He would have been like military leaders who died without a throne. (Acts 5:33-37) But Jesus conquered death, just as He said He would. (John 2:19-21) If there was no resurrection, Paul says, our faith would be worthless. We would be dead in our sins. (1 Cor. 15:17)

But Jesus' resurrection gives us hope for our resurrection. The same Spirit that raised Jesus from the dead will raise our bodies to life. (Rom. 8:11)

Jesus' crucifixion and resurrection are not the end of the story, but the center of it. As you teach kids this Bible story, emphasize the gospel: the good news of who Jesus is and what He has done. We do not worship a dead Savior. Jesus is alive! There is hope for sinners. Jesus' resurrection gives believers the promise of new life. "For as in Adam all die, so also in Christ all will be made alive" (1 Cor. 15:22).

The **BIBLE** Story

Jesus' Crucifixion and Resurrection
Matthew 26–28; 1 Corinthians 15

After Jesus was arrested, He was led to the high priest. The religious leaders were trying to find a reason to kill Jesus, but they could not. **The high priest asked, "Are You the Messiah, the Son of God?" Jesus replied, "Yes, that's right."**

The high priest said, "He has spoken against God! He deserves to die!" The religious leaders refused to believe that Jesus was God's Son.

In the morning, the religious leaders led Jesus to Pilate, the governor. "Are You the King of the Jews?" Pilate asked.

"Yes, that's right," Jesus replied.

"What should I do with Jesus?" Pilate asked the crowd. "Crucify Him!" they answered. Pilate did not think Jesus had done anything wrong, but he handed Jesus over and said, "Do whatever you want."

The governor's soldiers put a scarlet robe on Jesus. They made a crown of thorns and put it on His head. Then they mocked Him: "Here is the King of the Jews!" They beat Jesus and led Him away to be killed.

The soldiers nailed Jesus to a cross. They put a sign above His head that said THIS IS JESUS, THE KING OF THE JEWS. **Two**

criminals were crucified next to Him.

Darkness covered the land. **Jesus cried out, "My God, My God, why have You forsaken Me?" Jesus shouted again and then He died.** Suddenly, the curtain in the temple sanctuary split in two, from top to bottom, and there was an earthquake. One of the men guarding Jesus' body said, "This man really was God's Son!"

Jesus was buried in a tomb. A stone was sealed in front of the tomb so that no one could steal Jesus' body.

On the third day, Mary Magdalene (MAG duh leen) **and the other Mary went to the tomb.** Suddenly there was an earthquake. **An angel of the Lord rolled back the stone and sat on it.** The guards were so afraid that they fainted.

The angel spoke to the women, "Don't be afraid! I know you are looking for Jesus. He is not here. He has risen, just like He said He would."

The women left the tomb quickly. They **ran to tell the disciples the good news. Just then Jesus greeted them. The women worshiped Him. "Don't be afraid,"** Jesus **told them. "Tell My followers to go to Galilee. They will see Me there."**

Jesus appeared to Peter and then to the other disciples. Jesus also appeared to more than 500 people who followed Him. **Many people witnessed that Jesus is alive!**

Christ Connection: Jesus' death and resurrection is the center of the gospel. In Adam, we were spiritually dead in sin, but Jesus died to pay for our sins. Jesus is alive! God gives new life to everyone who trusts in Jesus.

Bible Storytelling Tips

- **Draw pictures:** Sketch symbols as you tell the story—a question mark for Jesus' trial, a cross for His death, a rising sun for His resurrection, and so on.
- **Use lighting effects:** Begin the story with lights dimmed. Raise the lights when telling of Jesus' resurrection.

INTRODUCE the Story

SESSION TITLE: Jesus' Crucifixion and Resurrection
BIBLE PASSAGE: Matthew 26–28; 1 Corinthians 15
STORY POINT: Jesus' resurrection gives us hope for eternal life.
KEY PASSAGE: John 3:30
BIG PICTURE QUESTION: Why did Jesus become human? Jesus became human to obey His Father's plan and rescue sinners.

Welcome time

Greet each kid as he or she arrives. Use this time to collect the offering, fill out attendance sheets, and help new kids connect to your group. Prompt kids to think about ways they can show love to their friends and family members. How can they tell if someone else loves them?

Activity page (5 minutes)

· "He's Alive!" activity page, 1 per kid
· pencils or markers

Invite kids to complete "He's Alive!" on the activity page. Guide kids to find the path from the cross to the tomb and then to Jesus.

SAY • Today's Bible story is about Jesus' journey from the cross to the grave and then out again! We will find out more about what happened.

Session starter (10 minutes)

OPTION 1: Silent sillies

Choose a kid to stand at the front of the room. Whisper a phrase in her ear and challenge her to act it out silently. The rest of the kids should shout out what they think is happening. When a kid guesses correctly, she gets to act out the next phrase. Play several rounds.

Suggested phrases: *playing baseball, delivering mail, landing an airplane, flying a kite, playing chess, baking bread, scuba diving, watering a garden, finger-painting, building a campfire, shopping at the mall, dancing a ballet*

SAY • Sometimes what you thought was happening and what was actually happening didn't quite match. In today's Bible story, we will hear about a time when people though Jesus had been defeated by His enemies. But that wasn't the true story.

OPTION 2: It's empty

Place a rock or paper wad beneath two of three inverted cups while the kids are watching. Try to confuse the kids by quickly rearranging the cups in front of them. After several seconds, ask the kids which cup they think is empty.

· rocks or paper wads, 2
· opaque cups, 3

To make the game more difficult, turn away from the kids and mix up the cups. Then ask one person to guess which cup is empty. Allow her to poll the rest of the group to see if they agree. Then lift the cup she chose to show whether or not it is empty. Play as time allows.

SAY • In the Bible story we will hear today, some of Jesus' friends went to the tomb and expected to find His body there. But the tomb was empty!

Transition to teach the story

TEACH the Story

SESSION TITLE: Jesus' Crucifixion and Resurrection
BIBLE PASSAGE: Matthew 26–28; 1 Corinthians 15
STORY POINT: Jesus' resurrection gives us hope for eternal life.
KEY PASSAGE: John 3:30
BIG PICTURE QUESTION: Why did Jesus become human? Jesus became human to obey His Father's plan and rescue sinners.

Countdown

· countdown video

Show the countdown video as you transition to teach the story. Set it to end as the session begins.

Introduce the session (3 minutes)

· leader attire
· bandanna
· Bible

Tip: If you prefer not to use themed content or characters, adapt or omit this introduction.

[Leader enters quickly, carrying a bandanna and a Bible. Leader wipes his or her forehead and appears out of breath.]

LEADER • Whew! I was not sure I was going to make it in today. I was driving along when all of a sudden I saw a large boulder roll off a cliff ahead of me, and it landed right in the roadway! Thankfully it didn't hit any cars! But the road was partially blocked until the department of transportation could come out and move the boulder. They used some powerful machinery to move it out of the way enough to get traffic flowing again. I can't imagine what people did before the invention of strong machines. There's no way a person could move a rock that big on his own.

You know, that makes me think of the Bible story we are going to hear today. This story happened more than two thousand years ago. It involves a large stone that was rolled away from the entrance of a tomb.

But no construction trucks were involved. Let's find
out what happened.

Big picture question (1 minute)

LEADER • Raise your hand if you remember our big picture
question. [*Call on a volunteer.*] That's right. **Why did
Jesus become human?** That's an important question
to think about because Jesus came to earth for us.
Why? Here's the answer: **Jesus became human to
obey His Father's plan and rescue sinners.** God the
Son didn't come down because we were so awesome
that He wanted to hang out with us; He loved us,
and we needed Him!

Giant timeline (1 minute)

Show the giant timeline. Point to individual Bible stories as
you review.

· Giant Timeline

LEADER • We are pausing in our timeline to hear today's
Bible story, but let's look back at some recent stories.
All the stories of the Bible actually point to the story
we are going to hear. We've been hearing about how
Jesus came into the world and how **Jesus obeyed
God by being baptized.** Jesus wanted to do God's
plan all along, and today's story—the story of Jesus'
death and resurrection—show how Jesus carried out
that plan.

Tell the Bible story (10 minutes)

Open your Bible to Matthew 26–28; 1 Corinthians 15.
Use the Bible storytelling tips on the Bible story page to
help you tell the story, or show the Bible story video "Jesus'
Crucifixion and Resurrection."

· Bibles
· "Jesus' Crucifixion
  and Resurrection"
  video
· Big Picture Question
  Poster
· Bible Story Picture
  Poster
· Story Point Poster

LEADER • Jesus was the solution for a very big problem: the problem of sin. Ever since sin entered the world with Adam and Eve, everything has been affected. Our sin separates us from God, and no matter how hard we try to be good or to do the right thing, we cannot get back to God on our own. And the Bible says the punishment for sin is death.

That's bad news. But when sin entered the world, God did not leave people on their own to suffer the consequences and die, separated from Him forever. He made a promise that He would send a Savior. God did. He sent His Son to be born into the world as a baby. Jesus grew up and taught people the truth about God. Some people believed Him, but many did not.

Jesus never sinned, but He was arrested and crucified on a cross. When Jesus died, He took the punishment we deserve for our sins—past, present, and future.

Then something amazing happened. On the third day, Jesus came to life again. Who went to visit Jesus' tomb? Look at Matthew 28:1. [*Allow kids to read the verse and respond.*] An angel told the women that Jesus had risen from the dead. Then Jesus appeared to the women! What did Jesus tell the women to do? Look at Matthew 28:10. [*Allow kids to read the verse and respond.*]

Christ connection

LEADER • Jesus showed that He has power over sin and death. God accepted Jesus' payment for sin, so everyone who trusts in Him can be forgiven and have

Tip: Use Scripture and the guide provided on page 109 to explain how to become a Christian. Make sure kids know when and where they can ask questions.

eternal life. **Jesus' resurrection gives us hope for eternal life.**

Jesus' death and resurrection is the center of the gospel. In Adam, we were spiritually dead in sin, but Jesus died to pay for our sins. Jesus is alive! God gives new life to everyone who trusts in Jesus.

Questions from kids video (3 minutes)

Show the "Easter, Session 2" questions from kids video. Prompt kids to consider why Jesus died. Guide them to discuss whether or not Christians should always forgive.

· "Easter, Session 2" questions from kids video

Missions moment (3 minutes)

Show "The Gospel" missions video and then ask kids to describe things we should tell other people about Jesus. (*He was born on earth, He died on a cross for our sins, He rose to life, He wants everyone to be with Him in heaven forever*)

· "The Gospel" missions video

LEADER •The gospel—the good news of Jesus—is the reason that missionaries go all over the world. They want to be obedient to take the gospel to all people, even those who are very hard to reach. Missionaries sacrifice so that others can hear about Jesus and know that Jesus' resurrection gives us hope for eternal life. Lead a brief prayer for missionaries your church supports.

Key passage (5 minutes)

Show the key passage poster. Lead the boys and girls to read together John 3:30.

· Key Passage Poster
· "He Must Increase, but I Must Decrease (John 3:30)" song

LEADER • When Jesus started His ministry, John the Baptist pointed people to Him. The King had come, and He was the very Word of God. At best, John could point people to Jesus, and say, "I am not Jesus! But look, there He is!" Jesus must increase because He is from heaven and is above all. He is the best and no one compares. Jesus spoke of what he had seen and heard from God the Father. Like John, we should say, "Jesus must increase!"

Lead boys and girls in singing "He Must Increase, but I Must Decrease (John 3:30)."

Sing (4 minutes)

Open your Bible and read aloud Hebrews 1:3.

LEADER • Jesus is amazing. Not only does He show us exactly what God is like, He holds everything together. He came to earth and paid the price for our sins by dying on the cross. He rose from the dead on the third day, later ascended into heaven, and then He sat down at the right hand of God the Father. He deserves our praise! Let's sing.

Sing together "Jesus Messiah."

Pray (2 minutes)

Invite kids to pray before dismissing to apply the story.

LEADER • Lord God, You are mighty. With Your power, You raised Jesus from the dead. We praise You, Jesus, because You have power over sin and death. Help us to remember the cross and the empty tomb every day. When we trust in You, You give us new life. We feel the effects of sin in the world, but we have hope of life with You forever. Give us boldness to share this good news with the world. We love You. Amen.

Dismiss to apply the story

· "Jesus Messiah" song
· Bible

The Gospel: God's Plan for Me

Ask kids if they have ever heard the word *gospel*. Clarify that the word *gospel* means "good news." It is the message about Christ, the kingdom of God, and salvation. Use the following guide to share the gospel with kids.

God rules. Explain to kids that the Bible tells us God created everything, and He is in charge of everything. Invite a volunteer to read Genesis 1:1 from the Bible. Read Revelation 4:11 or Colossians 1:16-17 aloud and explain what these verses mean.

We sinned. Tell kids that since the time of Adam and Eve, everyone has chosen to disobey God. (Romans 3:23) The Bible calls this sin. Because God is holy, God cannot be around sin. Sin separates us from God and deserves God's punishment of death. (Romans 6:23)

God provided. Choose a child to read John 3:16 aloud. Say that God sent His Son, Jesus, the perfect solution to our sin problem, to rescue us from the punishment we deserve. It's something we, as sinners, could never earn on our own. Jesus alone saves us. Read and explain Ephesians 2:8-9.

Jesus gives. Share with kids that Jesus lived a perfect life, died on the cross for our sins, and rose again. Because Jesus gave up His life for us, we can be welcomed into God's family for eternity. This is the best gift ever! Read Romans 5:8; 2 Corinthians 5:21; or 1 Peter 3:18.

We respond. Tell kids that they can respond to Jesus. Read Romans 10:9-10,13. Review these aspects of our response: Believe in your heart that Jesus alone saves you through what He's already done on the cross. Repent, turning from self and sin to Jesus. Tell God and others that your faith is in Jesus.

Offer to talk with any child who is interested in responding to Jesus. Provide *I'm a Christian Now!* for new Christians to take home and complete with their families.

APPLY the Story

SESSION TITLE: Jesus' Crucifixion and Resurrection
BIBLE PASSAGE: Matthew 26–28; 1 Corinthians 15
STORY POINT: Jesus' resurrection gives us hope for eternal life.
KEY PASSAGE: John 3:30
BIG PICTURE QUESTION: Why did Jesus become human? Jesus became human to obey His Father's plan and rescue sinners.

Key passage activity (5 minutes)

· Key Passage Poster
· sticky notes

Display the key passage poster. Lead kids in reading aloud John 3:30 together. Choose a volunteer to cover one of the words on the poster with a sticky note. Guide kids to say the key passage again, filling in the covered word from memory. Allow another volunteer to cover another word. Repeat until kids recite the key passage from memory.

SAY • Can anyone explain what these words mean? [*Allow kids to respond.*] John the Baptist was speaking to his followers who were asking questions about Jesus. John's mission was to get people ready for Jesus, so John wanted people to follow Jesus! ***Why did Jesus become human? Jesus became human to obey His Father's plan and rescue sinners.***

Discussion & Bible skills (10 minutes)

· Bibles, 1 per kid
· Story Point Poster

Distribute Bibles. Guide boys and girls to open their Bibles to 1 Corinthians 15. Explain that the apostle Paul wrote 1 Corinthians as a letter to believers in Corinth about 20 years after Jesus' death and resurrection. He wanted to remind believers what was true. Choose a volunteer to read aloud 1 Corinthians 15:3-5.

Older Kids Leader Guide
Easter • Session 2

SAY • In these verses, Paul shares the gospel—the good
news about Jesus. This is the most important news
ever! Jesus died for our sins, He was buried, and He
was raised on the third day.

Ask the following questions. Lead the group to discuss:

Option: Retell or review the Bible story using the bolded text of the Bible story script.

1. Why is it important that Jesus didn't stay dead but
He came back to life? *Lead kids to recognize that Jesus'
resurrection proved that God accepted Jesus' death as the
payment for sin. It shows His victory over sin and death.
Paul said if there was no resurrection, we would still be
dead in our sins. (1 Cor. 15:17) Jesus' resurrection gives
us hope that we too will be resurrected one day.*
(Option: Choose a volunteer to read Rom. 8:11.)

2. How do we know Jesus is alive? Where is He today?
*Guide kids to recall that after Jesus rose from the dead,
He appeared to the women and the twelve disciples as
well as more than 500 other people. Emphasize that we
ultimately believe by faith in Jesus' resurrection. Today,
Jesus is alive in heaven. One day, He will return to set
up His kingdom forever.*
(Option: Choose a volunteer to read Acts 7:55-56.)

3. How does the fact that Jesus' tomb is empty affect
how we live today? *Prompt kids to consider the reality
that Jesus has conquered sin and death, providing
forgiveness to all who trust in Him. The empty tomb
shows that God is faithful, powerful, and loving.
Because Jesus is alive, we can live with confidence that
our future with Him is secure.* **Jesus' resurrection
gives us hope for eternal life.** *We can live with a
purpose—to know God and make Him known. We
have hope even in hard circumstances.*
(Option: Choose a kid to read 1 Cor. 15:57-58.)

Activity choice (10 minutes)

- small clay or plastic flower pots, 1 per kid
- stickers
- markers

OPTION 1: Make a flower pot

If your church participates in a missions offering at Easter, like the Annie Armstrong Easter Offering, tell your kids about your church's role in giving to missions this time of year. Giving even small offerings is one way that kids can be involved in supporting missions.

Distribute pots and invite kids to decorate a flower pot to use at home to collect coins.

Tip: Use this activity option to reinforce the missions moment from Teach the Story.

Note: Consider asking parents or church members to donate travel-size toiletry items for a mission project included in session 3 of this unit.

SAY • Giving money is one way that we can support missionaries. That's why our church gives offerings to missions. We help to provide things like food, transportation, housing, and Bibles in different languages. It's one way that we can help missionaries who share the message of Jesus' death and resurrection with people who do not know.

Suggest that kids collect coins over the next month and add their offerings to the flower pots. Plan a time of collecting their offerings and presenting them to the church to use for missions.

LOW PREP

- poster board, 5 pieces
- crayons, markers, or colored pencils
- Bibles
- Gospel Plan Poster

OPTION 2: Gospel plan posters

Form five groups of kids. Give each group a piece of poster board; a copy of the Gospel Plan Poster; a Bible; and crayons, markers, or colored pencils. Review the gospel plan with kids. Then assign each group one of the sections on the poster:

1. God rules.
2. We sinned.
3. God provided.
4. Jesus gives.
5. We respond.

Instruct each group to design a poster featuring their section's logo, heading, and words from the Scripture passage. Then invite groups to share their posters in order.

SAY • *Gospel* means "good news!" Jesus' death and resurrection is the center of the gospel. We are born into Adam's family as sinners. In Adam, we were spiritually dead in sin, but Jesus died to pay for our sins. Jesus is alive! God adopts us into His family and gives new life to everyone who trusts in Jesus.

Option: Review the gospel with boys and girls. Explain that kids are welcome to speak with you or another teacher if they have questions.

Journal and prayer (5 minutes)

Distribute journal pages and pencils. Guide kids to think about and answer the questions listed on the page:

- What does this story teach me about God or the gospel?
- What does the story teach me about myself?
- Are there any commands in this story to obey? How are they for God's glory and my good?
- Are there any promises in this story to remember? How do they help me trust and love God?
- How does this story help me to live on mission better?

· pencils
· Journal Page
· "Easter Scramble" activity page, 1 per kid

As kids journal, invite them to share their ideas. Then pray, thanking God for the gift of salvation through His Son and for the hope of life with Him forever.

As time allows, lead kids to complete "Easter Scramble" on the activity page. Kids should unscramble the key words from today's Bible story.

Tip: Give parents this week's *Big Picture Cards for Families* to allow families to interact with the biblical content at home.

Unit 20 · Session 2
Jesus' Temptation

BIBLE PASSAGE:
Matthew 4; Mark 1; Luke 4

STORY POINT:
Jesus was tempted and never sinned.

KEY PASSAGE:
John 3:30

BIG PICTURE QUESTION:
Why did Jesus become human?
Jesus became human to obey His
Father's plan and rescue sinners.

INTRODUCE THE STORY	TEACH THE STORY	APPLY THE STORY
(10–15 MINUTES)	(25–30 MINUTES)	(25–30 MINUTES)
PAGE 118	**PAGE 120**	**PAGE 126**

 →  →

Additional resources are available at gospelproject.com. For free training and session-by-session help, visit ministrygrid.com/gospelproject.

LEADER Bible Study

Satan wants to ruin God's plan. In Genesis 3, he tempted Adam and Eve to disobey God. Sin entered the world, and the perfect relationship between God and man was broken. But all along, God had a plan to rescue His people through His Son. So when Jesus came to earth, Satan didn't back down. After Jesus was baptized—beginning His ministry and effectively declaring war on Satan—Satan tempted Jesus.

If Satan could just get Jesus to stray from God's perfect plan—if he could just get Jesus to sin—then Jesus would be disqualified to be the sinless Savior people needed. But Satan could not stop God's plan.

Jesus' temptation is not primarily an example to be followed but more a declaration of who Jesus is. He is the answer to God's promise of a descendant who would crush the head of the snake. (Gen. 3:15) Jesus is the perfect sacrifice required to take away sin. Where Adam failed, Jesus succeeded. Adam brought guilt and death to the human race, but Jesus brings forgiveness and life to all who trust in Him.

Even today, the devil works hard "to steal and kill and destroy" (John 10:10). Teach kids that the power to resist temptation comes from Jesus. Kids may struggle to understand that following Jesus won't mean instant eradication of sin and temptation in our lives. (Sanctification is a lifelong process!) Pray that the kids you teach would see Jesus as their greatest treasure— more valuable than any instant gratification the world has to offer.

Finally, give kids hope for when they fail. Jesus' perfect obedience is credited to those who trust in Him. Remind the kids that "if we confess our sins, he [God] is faithful and righteous to forgive us our sins and to cleanse us from all unrighteousness" (1 John 1:9). We can boldly approach God's throne to receive both grace and mercy when we need it. (See Heb. 4:14-16.)

The **BIBLE** Story

Jesus' Temptation

Matthew 4; Mark 1; Luke 4

After Jesus was baptized, the Holy Spirit led Him into the wilderness to be tempted by the devil. Jesus did not eat for 40 days and 40 nights. He prayed and thought about God's plan for His life. When those days were over, Jesus was hungry.

Then the devil, who tempts people to sin, came up to Jesus. He said, "If You are really God's Son, prove it. Tell these stones to become bread."

If Jesus used His power to turn the stones into bread, He could eat them so He wouldn't be hungry anymore. But Jesus refused. **Instead of using His own power, Jesus chose to trust God to meet His needs. Jesus said, "God's Word says that man must not live on bread alone but on every word that comes from the mouth of God."**

The devil tempted Jesus again. He took Jesus to the top of the temple in Jerusalem and said, "If You are really God's Son, prove it. Jump off this temple and trust God to protect You."

The devil even said: "God's Word says that God will order His angels to keep You safe, and they will protect You so that You will not even strike your foot against a stone."

The devil had used words from Scripture, but Jesus knew the devil's

Older Kids Leader Guide
Unit 20 • Session 2

command was foolish. **Jesus reminded him, "God's Word also says, do not test the Lord your God."**

Finally, the devil took Jesus to a high mountain. He showed Jesus all the kingdoms of the world and how great they were. The devil said to Jesus, "I will give You all the riches and power of these kingdoms. They belong to me, and I can give them to anyone I want. If You want them, **all You have to do is fall down and worship me."**

Jesus resisted temptation again. He replied, "Go away, Satan! God's Word says: Worship the Lord your God and serve Him only."

The devil left Jesus, and angels came right away to serve Jesus. Throughout all these temptations, **Jesus never sinned.**

Christ Connection: Jesus was tempted, but He trusted God and never sinned. Jesus is perfect and righteous. A perfect sacrifice was required to take away sin. Jesus was that perfect sacrifice. He died on the cross to free us from sin and to give us the power to say no to temptation.

Bible Storytelling Tips

- **Display a prop:** Each time you tell how Jesus responded to temptation, hold up the Bible.
- **Use dramatic conversation:** During dialogue, stand in various places for each speaker—Jesus and the devil.

INTRODUCE the Story

SESSION TITLE: Jesus' Temptation

BIBLE PASSAGE: Matthew 4; Mark 1; Luke 4

STORY POINT: Jesus was tempted and never sinned.

KEY PASSAGE: John 3:30

BIG PICTURE QUESTION: Why did Jesus become human? Jesus became human to obey His Father's plan and rescue sinners.

Welcome time

Greet each kid as he or she arrives. Use this time to collect the offering, fill out attendance sheets, and help new kids connect to your group. Prompt kids to talk about how they decide if something is right or wrong. Have they ever known what the right thing to do was, but still wanted to do something different? What happened?

Activity page (5 minutes)

- "What Would You Do?" activity page, 1 per kid
- pencils or markers

Invite kids to complete "What Would You Do?" on the activity page. Guide kids to read each scenario and circle how they would respond.

SAY • Do you always choose to do what is right? Why or why not? [*Invite kids to share.*] In the Bible story we will hear today, Jesus was tempted. To *tempt* someone is to try to get him or her to make a wrong choice or do something that is wrong. We'll find out what Jesus did when He faced temptation.

LOW PREP

- index cards
- paper
- markers or colored pencils

Session starter (10 minutes)

OPTION 1: Say what?

Before the session, list common English idioms on separate

index cards. Prepare one per kid or, if your group is large, one per group of two to four kids.

Distribute the prepared index cards along with paper and markers or colored pencils. Instruct kids to read the phrase on their cards and then illustrate what it could mean literally. For example, *missed the boat* means "it's too late" but might be illustrated as someone standing on shore as a boat pulls away.

SAY • Have you ever heard a phrase used in a way it wasn't intended to be used? Saying someone spilled the beans usually doesn't mean he literally spilled beans; it means he told a secret. In today's Bible story, we'll see one way someone tried to use God's words in a way they weren't meant to be used.

Examples of idioms:
- a blessing in disguise
- cutting corners
- hang in there
- on the ball
- pull yourself together
- under the weather
- a perfect storm
- break the ice
- spill the beans
- elephant in the room
- on the fence
- seeing eye to eye

OPTION 2: Obstacle course

Create a simple obstacle course with items you have available. Arrange cones or chairs for kids to weave through or step over. Position hula hoops for kids to jump into and out of, run around, or crawl through. You may use masking tape to mark a zig-zag path or hopscotch pattern on the floor. Before kids begin, demonstrate how to navigate the obstacles. Invite kids to take turns completing the course.

- cones or chairs
- hula hoops
- masking tape or painter's tape

SAY • Sometimes obstacles come up in life that try to keep us from following Jesus. The devil is against God and those who love God. The devil might tempt us to sin against God, but Jesus gives us power to resist temptation. Today we are going to hear a Bible story about a time Jesus was tempted.

Transition to teach the story

TEACH the Story

SESSION TITLE: Jesus' Temptation
BIBLE PASSAGE: Matthew 4; Mark 1; Luke 4
STORY POINT: Jesus was tempted and never sinned.
KEY PASSAGE: John 3:30
BIG PICTURE QUESTION: Why did Jesus become human? Jesus became human to obey His Father's plan and rescue sinners.

Countdown

· countdown video

Show the countdown video as you transition to teach the story. Set it to end as the session begins.

Introduce the session (3 minutes)

· leader attire
· stop sign
· message board

[Leader enters wearing khaki pants, a reflective shirt or vest, and a hard hat. Leader carries a stop sign made from poster board attached to a tall broomstick. A traffic message board reads DANGER AHEAD.*]*

Tip: If you prefer not to use themed content or characters, adapt or omit this introduction.

LEADER • Whoa! Hold up, everyone. Do you see that sign there? It says *Danger Ahead*. I think it would be a good idea if you all stopped here for a bit while we assess the situation. When it's safe to proceed, you can move on with caution. OK?

Hey, haven't I seen you here before? Yeah! I remember now. Some of you are frequent travelers through these parts. Well, in case you forgot, I'm [*your name*]. My job is traffic control while some construction is happening just down the road. I know construction can be inconvenient, but when these improvements are made, the delay will be worth it. While we wait, let me tell you a Bible story.

Older Kids Leader Guide
Unit 20 • Session 2

Big picture question (1 minute)

LEADER • As you listen, keep a big picture question in mind. Big picture questions help us to think about what God is up to. Our question is, *why did Jesus become human?* Here is the answer: *Jesus became human to obey His Father's plan and rescue sinners.* Now I'll ask the question, and you say the answer: *Why did Jesus become human?* [*Let kids respond.*] *Jesus became human to obey His Father's plan and rescue sinners.* That was great!

Giant timeline (1 minute)

Show the giant timeline. Point to individual Bible stories as you review.

· Giant Timeline

LEADER • Today's Bible story and the stories that happen before and after it have to do with Jesus getting ready for His ministry on earth. We heard about Jesus' baptism. **Jesus obeyed God by being baptized.**

Baptism reminds us of Jesus' death and resurrection. It reminds us that when we trust in Jesus, we turn from sin and start a new life—a life lived for Jesus. Today's Bible story is called "Jesus' Temptation." Let's find out what happened.

Tell the Bible story (10 minutes)

Open your Bible to Matthew 4; Mark 1; Luke 4. Use the Bible storytelling tips on the Bible story page to help you tell the story, or show the Bible story video "Jesus' Temptation."

· Bibles
· "Jesus' Temptation" video
· Big Picture Question Poster
· Bible Story Picture Poster
· Story Point Poster

LEADER • Do you remember anyone else who was tempted by the devil? Adam and Eve were tempted, and they did sin. When sin entered the world, everything was affected. We are all sinners, and we need Jesus.

Do you know why the devil wanted to get Jesus to sin? The devil is against God and His perfect plan. If Jesus sinned, then He couldn't be the sinless Savior people needed. But the devil could not stop God's plan. **Jesus was tempted and never sinned.**

Think about the things the devil tried to get Jesus to do: He wanted Jesus to use His own power to meet His own needs. Jesus hadn't eaten in 40 days. He was hungry! Did Jesus sin? No. What did Jesus say? Look at Matthew 4:4. [*Allow kids to read the verse and respond.*]

The devil wanted Jesus to test God by jumping off the temple. Did Jesus sin? No. What did Jesus say? Look at Matthew 4:7. [*Allow kids to read the verse and respond.*] Finally, the devil offered Jesus kingdoms to rule over if Jesus would worship him. Did Jesus sin? No! What did Jesus say? Look at Matthew 4:10. [*Allow kids to read the verse and respond.*]

The Bible says that before we trust in Jesus, we are slaves to sin. Sin has power over us. Jesus came to be the perfect sacrifice required to take away sin. He died on the cross and rose again to free us from sin and to give us the power to say no to temptation. That is such great news!

Christ connection

LEADER • Jesus was tempted in the wilderness. Do you remember a time when God's people—the Israelites—were in the wilderness? After God delivered His people from Egypt, they traveled into the wilderness and rebelled against God. They worshiped idols and complained. God punished the people by making them wander for 40 years. When Jesus was in the wilderness, He obeyed God perfectly. Jesus is perfect and righteous. A perfect sacrifice was required to pay for our sins so we could have forgiveness and life with God forever. Jesus was that perfect sacrifice. He died on the cross to free us from sin and to give us the power to say no to temptation.

Tip: Use Scripture and the guide provided on page 125 to explain how to become a Christian. Make sure kids know when and where they can ask questions.

Questions from kids video (3 minutes)

Show the "Unit 20, Session 2" questions from kids video. Prompt kids to think about how Jesus was tempted. Guide them to discuss how we can recognize if we are being tempted and how to fight temptation.

· "Unit 20, Session 2" questions from kids video

Missions moment (3 minutes)

LEADER • I want to introduce you to a great woman of faith. Betty Greene was the first female missionary pilot. She helped to start the Mission Aviation Fellowship (MAF) that uses small airplanes to reach people in remote villages. MAF helps people and shares the stories of Jesus, like the one we're learning: **Jesus was tempted but never sinned.** Let's hear more about Betty Greene.

Ask a volunteer to read the story of Betty Greene. Display the photos and give kids the chance to look at them. Then pray, thanking God for missionaries like Betty Greene and for missionary pilots today.

· "Betty Greene Photos" printable
· "Betty Greene Story" printable

Key passage (5 minutes)

Show the key passage poster. Lead the boys and girls to read together John 3:30.

· Key Passage Poster
· "He Must Increase, but I Must Decrease (John 3:30)" song

LEADER • In a world where popularity and influence are highly valued, we can be tempted to steal God's glory to increase our own fame instead of His. But John the Baptist recognized Jesus as the One who deserves all glory and honor. We can echo John's words about Jesus: "He must increase, but I must decrease."

Lead kids to sing "He Must Increase, but I Must Decrease (John 3:30)."

Sing (4 minutes)

Open your Bible and read aloud Hebrews 4:15-16.

LEADER • Jesus knows what it is like to be tempted. **Jesus was tempted and never sinned.** He died on the cross to free us from sin and to give us the power to say no to temptation. We can go to Him in prayer—without fear and shame—because He is gracious and will help us. Let's sing.

Sing together "Take It to the Lord."

Pray (2 minutes)

Invite kids to pray before dismissing to apply the story.

LEADER • Father, Your Word is powerful. Jesus remembered the truth of Scripture when the devil tempted Him to sin. Help us remember Your Word. Call to mind the truth when we are tempted to believe lies about who You are and who we are. Lord, we confess that we fall short and give in to temptation. We trust in Jesus, who never sinned. Forgive us and strengthen us. We want to honor You with our lives. We love You. Amen.

Dismiss to apply the story

· "Take It to the Lord" song
· Bible

The Gospel: God's Plan for Me

Ask kids if they have ever heard the word *gospel*. Clarify that the word *gospel* means "good news." It is the message about Christ, the kingdom of God, and salvation. Use the following guide to share the gospel with kids.

God rules. Explain to kids that the Bible tells us God created everything, and He is in charge of everything. Invite a volunteer to read Genesis 1:1 from the Bible. Read Revelation 4:11 or Colossians 1:16-17 aloud and explain what these verses mean.

We sinned. Tell kids that since the time of Adam and Eve, everyone has chosen to disobey God. (Romans 3:23) The Bible calls this sin. Because God is holy, God cannot be around sin. Sin separates us from God and deserves God's punishment of death. (Romans 6:23)

God provided. Choose a child to read John 3:16 aloud. Say that God sent His Son, Jesus, the perfect solution to our sin problem, to rescue us from the punishment we deserve. It's something we, as sinners, could never earn on our own. Jesus alone saves us. Read and explain Ephesians 2:8-9.

Jesus gives. Share with kids that Jesus lived a perfect life, died on the cross for our sins, and rose again. Because Jesus gave up His life for us, we can be welcomed into God's family for eternity. This is the best gift ever! Read Romans 5:8; 2 Corinthians 5:21; or 1 Peter 3:18.

We respond. Tell kids that they can respond to Jesus. Read Romans 10:9-10,13. Review these aspects of our response: Believe in your heart that Jesus alone saves you through what He's already done on the cross. Repent, turning from self and sin to Jesus. Tell God and others that your faith is in Jesus.

Offer to talk with any child who is interested in responding to Jesus. Provide *I'm a Christian Now!* for new Christians to take home and complete with their families.

APPLY the Story

SESSION TITLE: Jesus' Temptation
BIBLE PASSAGE: Matthew 4; Mark 1; Luke 4
STORY POINT: Jesus was tempted and never sinned.
KEY PASSAGE: John 3:30
BIG PICTURE QUESTION: Why did Jesus become human? Jesus became human to obey His Father's plan and rescue sinners.

Key passage activity (5 minutes)

· Key Passage Poster
· index cards
· marker

Display the key passage poster. Lead kids in reading aloud John 3:30 together. Provide index cards and markers. Instruct kids to write the words of the key passage on separate index cards—one or two words per card. Challenge kids to mix up the cards and arrange them in order again. Kids may choose to trade sets with a friend and continue practicing. As kids master the verse, let them race other kids to see who can arrange the words the fastest.

SAY • Good job, everyone. Can you think of some reasons why Jesus should increase and we should decrease? [*Allow kids to respond.*]

We have a choice to make about who will be on the throne of our lives. The devil will tempt us to live for ourselves instead of Jesus. We can turn from self and sin and turn to Jesus.

Discussion & Bible skills (10 minutes)

· Bibles, 1 per kid
· Story Point Poster
· Small Group Timeline and Map Set (005802970)

Distribute Bibles. Guide boys and girls to open their Bibles to Matthew 4. Explain that today's Bible story is found in Matthew 4:1-11.

SAY • Raise your hand if you have ever been tempted. Keep your hand raised if you have ever said no to sin. Now put your hand down if you have ever failed and sinned.

The Bible says that **Jesus was tempted and never sinned.** Jesus is different than us. *Why did Jesus become human? Jesus became human to obey His Father's plan and rescue sinners.* That's good news!

Jesus knows how hard it can be to say no to sin. When we are tempted to sin, we can pray and ask Him to help us say no to sin.

Choose a volunteer to read aloud Matthew 4:3-4. Ask the following questions. Lead the group to discuss:

1. Who tempts us to sin? Why? *Lead kids to recall that the devil tempted Jesus to sin. Assure them that God never tempts anyone to sin. Explain that the Bible says the devil is "the father of lies" (John 8:44). The devil is against everything that God loves. He might tempt us to sin because He does not want us to follow Jesus.*
(Option: Choose a volunteer to read James 1:13-14.)

2. How can we resist temptation? What should we do if we give in to temptation? *Lead kids to discuss how Jesus resisted temptation—by remembering the truth found in Scripture. Encourage kids to memorize Scripture and pray against the schemes of the devil. Emphasize that when we are tempted, God provides a way to resist it. When we do sin, we can repent and turn back to God. He will forgive our sins.*
(Option: Choose a volunteer to read 1 Cor. 10:13.)

3. Why is it important to know God's Word? *Invite kids to discuss the importance of knowing what is true about God and about ourselves. We are often tempted when we believe lies about God or ourselves. Knowing God's*

Option: Retell or review the Bible story using the bolded text of the Bible story script.

Word and treasuring it in our hearts can help us stand up against temptation.

(Option: Choose a volunteer to read Ps. 119:9-11.)

Activity choice (10 minutes)

LOW PREP

· paper

Tip: Use this activity option to reinforce the missions moment from Teach the Story.

OPTION 1: Make paper airplanes

Distribute paper and encourage kids to make their best paper airplanes. Consider downloading some simple paper airplane patterns from the Internet for those who need extra help. Let the kids have a contest to see which airplane travels the farthest.

SAY • These paper airplanes can remind us to pray for missionary pilots like the ones with MAF. They can reach people in mountain villages, deep jungles, or remote islands that no one else can get to. Their willingness to serve God means people will be helped and hear about Jesus.

Note: Consider asking parents or church members to donate travel-size toiletry items for a mission project included in session 3 of this unit.

· "Temptation Cards" printable

Option: Review the gospel with boys and girls. Explain that kids are welcome to speak with you or another teacher if they have questions.

OPTION 2: Practice resisting

Form four groups of kids. Give each group a temptation scenario card and give groups a couple of minutes to plan how they will act out the scenario.

Call on groups one at a time to act out their scenario. Before the scene resolves, direct the actors to freeze. Lead all of the kids to discuss a right and wrong response. Then let kids act out the response showing a person resisting temptation. Repeat for each scenario.

SAY • *Why did Jesus become human? Jesus became human to obey His Father's plan and rescue sinners.* When

Jesus came to earth, He experienced temptation just like we do. **Jesus was tempted and never sinned.**

Just like the devil tried to trick Jesus to sin, the devil wants us to sin too. The Bible says that when we resist the devil, he will go away. [*See James 4:7.*] We can turn to God for help to say no to sin. God gives us power through the Holy Spirit to resist temptation.

Journal and prayer (5 minutes)

Distribute journal pages and pencils. Guide kids to think about and answer the questions listed on the page:

- What does this story teach me about God or the gospel?
- What does the story teach me about myself?
- Are there any commands in this story to obey? How are they for God's glory and my good?
- Are there any promises in this story to remember? How do they help me trust and love God?
- How does this story help me to live on mission better?

As kids journal, invite them to share their ideas. Then pray, thanking God for His Word. Praise Jesus for resisting temptation and pray that God would help kids hide His Word in their hearts so they can use it to resist the devil.

As time allows, lead kids to complete "Temptation & Reply" on the activity page.

· pencils
· Journal Page
· "Temptation & Reply" activity page, 1 per kid

Tip: Give parents this week's *Big Picture Cards for Families* to allow families to interact with the biblical content at home.

Unit 20 · Session 3
John Pointed to Jesus

BIBLE PASSAGE:
Matthew 3; John 1; 3

STORY POINT:
John the Baptist told people
to follow Jesus.

KEY PASSAGE:
John 3:30

BIG PICTURE QUESTION:
Why did Jesus become human?
Jesus became human to obey His
Father's plan and rescue sinners.

INTRODUCE THE STORY
(10–15 MINUTES)
PAGE 134

→

TEACH THE STORY
(25–30 MINUTES)
PAGE 136

→

APPLY THE STORY
(25–30 MINUTES)
PAGE 142

Additional resources are available at gospelproject.com. For free training and session-by-session help, visit ministrygrid.com/gospelproject.

LEADER Bible Study

Hundreds of years before Jesus was born, the prophets had spoken of a forerunner—someone who would get people ready for Jesus. (Isa. 40:3; Mal. 3:1) At just the right time, "John came baptizing in the wilderness and proclaiming a baptism of repentance for the forgiveness of sins" (Mark 1:4). These baptisms were an outward sign of cleansing for people who had repented of their sins.

John's followers were concerned when they saw Jesus and His disciples, who were baptizing people too. They came to John, who pointed out several things about himself and about Jesus. Consider these comparisons as John explained that Jesus was greater than John.

First, who were they? John was clear: "I am not the Messiah" (John 3:28). John was not the bridegroom, but the groom's friend. Jesus is the bridegroom. (John 3:29)

Where did they come from? John was from the earth, and he belonged to the earth. Jesus comes from above and is above all. (John 3:31)

What did they do? John said, "He must increase, but I must decrease." John was a witness to the Light. (John 1:7-8) He was a voice in the wilderness, and Jesus is the Word. (John 1:14,23) John the Baptist told people to get ready for the Messiah. He baptized with water, but Jesus baptized with the Spirit. (John 1:33)

Finally, why were they here? John went before Jesus and rejoiced with Him. (John 3:28-29) Jesus came to give eternal life. (John 3:36)

John described his joy as being complete. (John 3:29) The One for whom he had prepared the people was here. The time had come for John to step aside and let Jesus take the spotlight. John's mission was complete.

The **BIBLE** Story

John Pointed to Jesus
Matthew 3; John 1; 3

Jesus and His disciples went out into the countryside. People came to see them, and Jesus taught the people. Many people were baptized.

Nearby, John the Baptist was baptizing people too. Some of the people who followed John got into an argument. They went to John. "Teacher," they said, "remember the man you talked about, the One who was with you on the other side of the Jordan River? His disciples are baptizing people, and people are starting to follow Him."

John's followers were talking about Jesus. John answered them, "You heard me say that I am not the Messiah. I am the messenger who goes before Him to announce that He is coming." This was true. John had said, "Someone greater than me is coming. I am not worthy to remove His sandals. I baptize you with water, but He will baptize you with the Holy Spirit."

John tried to explain by talking about a wedding. When two people get married, the man who marries the bride is the groom. His friend stands with him at the wedding, and he is happy to be there and hear the groom's voice. John also knew that a wedding is the groom's special day; **the groom's friend should not make it about himself. This was how John felt—like a groom's friend—because he was happy that Jesus, the Messiah, had come. John said, "Jesus must increase, but I must decrease."**

Then John explained why Jesus was more important than himself. John was from the earth, and he could only talk about things on earth. Jesus—the One who comes from heaven—talked about things in heaven because He had seen them! Still, no one believed what Jesus said.

Whoever believes Jesus knows that God tells the truth. God sent Jesus to earth, and Jesus speaks God's words.

The Father loves the Son and has given Him power over everything. Whoever believes in the Son will have eternal life, but whoever refuses to believe in the Son will not have eternal life. He will never be able to get away from God's judgment.

Christ Connection: John the Baptist told people to get ready for Jesus, the promised Messiah. Now that Jesus was on earth, John's mission was complete. Jesus was greater than John, and John joyfully stepped aside as Jesus began His earthly ministry.

Bible Storytelling Tips

- **Use sound effects:** Play sound effects of a river as you tell the story.
- **Make a T-chart:** List words John used to describe himself and Jesus (*not the Messiah/Messiah, groom's friend/groom,* and so on).

INTRODUCE the Story

SESSION TITLE: John Pointed to Jesus
BIBLE PASSAGE: Matthew 3; John 1; 3
STORY POINT: John the Baptist told people to follow Jesus.
KEY PASSAGE: John 3:30
BIG PICTURE QUESTION: Why did Jesus become human? Jesus became human to obey His Father's plan and rescue sinners.

Welcome time

Greet each kid as he or she arrives. Use this time to collect the offering, fill out attendance sheets, and help new kids connect to your group. Prompt kids to share something they witnessed this week. Did anyone else witness it?

Activity page (5 minutes)

· "On the Line" activity page, 1 per kid
· pencils or markers

Invite kids to complete "On the Line" on the activity page. Guide kids to mark each item on the scale to indicate how important it is to them. Invite volunteers to share which items they consider to be of greater importance than others.

SAY • How can you tell what is most important in someone's life? How do you show what is most important in your life? In the Bible story we will hear today, John the Baptist declared that it was time for him to step aside because someone greater had come.

Session starter (10 minutes)

OPTION 1: Circle name game
Instruct kids to stand in a circle. Stand in the center. Quickly go around the circle, calling for kids to say their own names so all kids are familiar with who is next to them

Explain that you will point to someone in the circle and will either say "you," "me," "left," or "right." Then you will begin counting to five. The person you point to should respond with the name of the person indicated. ("You" is the person pointed to, "me" is the person in the center, "left" is the person to the left of the person pointed to, and "right" is the person to the right of the person pointed to.)

If the person gives the correct name within five seconds, he becomes the pointer. If not, the pointer remains in the middle for a new round. Play multiple rounds.

SAY • Today we are going to hear about John the Baptist and Jesus. People followed John the Baptist and learned from him. All along, John pointed to Jesus. He got people ready for Him. Jesus is greater than John. So when Jesus began His ministry, John essentially said, "Don't follow me; follow Him!"

OPTION 2: Where are you from?

Display a map. Invite kids to point to their hometowns, or provide small stickers to mark where they are from.

· map
· stickers (optional)

Allow kids to share about the places they marked on the map. Who has lived the farthest away? Who has always lived in your current city? Do they know anyone from another state or another country?

As time allows, lead kids to discuss other places they have traveled or places they would like to visit someday.

SAY • Today's Bible story is about Jesus and John. John explained to his followers who Jesus is and where He came from. Let's find out what John said.

Transition to teach the story

TEACH the Story

SESSION TITLE: John Pointed to Jesus
BIBLE PASSAGE: Matthew 3; John 1; 3
STORY POINT: John the Baptist told people to follow Jesus.
KEY PASSAGE: John 3:30
BIG PICTURE QUESTION: Why did Jesus become human? Jesus became human to obey His Father's plan and rescue sinners.

Countdown

· countdown video

Show the countdown video as you transition to teach the story. Set it to end as the session begins.

Introduce the session (3 minutes)

· leader attire
· stop sign
· message board
· Bible

[Leader enters wearing khaki pants, a reflective shirt or vest, and a hard hat. Leader carries a stop sign made from poster board attached to a tall broomstick. A traffic message board reads MERGE RIGHT. *Position a Bible nearby.]*

Tip: If you prefer not to use themed content or characters, adapt or omit this introduction.

LEADER • Hello! I'm [*your name*]. Please use caution; traffic is merging. Oh, wait a second. I recognize you! I am so glad to see you again! I'd love to chat, just let me make sure there's no more traffic. [*Look off into the distance and then set down the stop sign.*] All clear. Great! Whew, we had a bit of a rough day yesterday. You see, we had to close one of the lanes while construction is being completed, so all eastbound traffic needs to merge at this point. The crew painted a big arrow on the road to alert drivers, but it seems some people just don't pay attention or no one has ever taught them how to properly merge!

Anyway, did any of you bring your Bible today? I

know mine is around here somewhere … [*Pick up a Bible.*] Here it is! I can't wait to share today's Bible story with you. Are you ready?

Big picture question (1 minute)

LEADER • Let's review our big picture question: **Why did Jesus become human?** Our answer focuses on two reasons: **Jesus became human to** [*hold up one finger*] **obey His Father's plan and** [*hold up a second finger*] **rescue sinners.**

I'll ask the question, and then you say the answer: **Why did Jesus become human? Jesus became human to obey His Father's plan and rescue sinners.**

Giant timeline (1 minute)

Show the giant timeline. Point to individual Bible stories as you review.

· Giant Timeline

LEADER • We've been hearing stories about Jesus when He was around 30 years old. His ministry on earth was just getting started.

John the Baptist had been telling people to get ready for Jesus. John was baptizing people at the Jordan River when Jesus came to him and was baptized. Jesus never sinned, but **Jesus obeyed God by being baptized.** Then Jesus was led into the wilderness, where He was tempted by the devil. **Jesus was tempted and never sinned.**

Today's Bible story is called "John Pointed to Jesus." The time had come for John to step aside for Jesus to take center stage.

Tell the Bible story (10 minutes)

Open your Bible to Matthew 3; John 1; 3. Use the Bible storytelling tips on the Bible story page to help you tell the story, or show the Bible story video "John Pointed to Jesus."

LEADER • As John told people that the Messiah was coming and called them to repent and turn away from their sin, people began to follow John. John's followers were people who learned from him as he told people to get ready for Jesus. One day, they noticed that people were following this man named Jesus instead of following John. What was going on?

John explained to his followers who he was and who Jesus is. John said, "I am not the Messiah." John did not want his followers to look to him for salvation; he wanted them to look to Jesus. John could not save people from their sins. His job was to announce that the Messiah—the One who has the power to save people—was coming.

John pointed out how Jesus was different from John. What did John say? Look at Matthew 3:11. [*Allow kids to read the verse and respond.*] John said Jesus is more powerful. John baptized people with water to show that they were sorry for their sin, but he said Jesus would baptize people with the Holy Spirit. Jesus would change people's hearts!

What event did John talk about to explain how Jesus is greater? Look at John 3:29. [*Allow kids to read the verse and respond.*] John said that Jesus was like the groom at a wedding, and John was like the groom's friend. Everyone knows the groom at a wedding is more important than the groom's friend. **John the Baptist told people to follow Jesus.** He

said that Jesus came from heaven, and only Jesus can
save people from their sins.

Christ connection

LEADER • John the Baptist told people to get ready for
Jesus, the promised Messiah. Now that Jesus was on
earth, John's mission was complete. Jesus was greater
than John, and John joyfully stepped aside as Jesus
began His earthly ministry.

Tip: Use Scripture
and the guide
provided on page
141 to explain
how to become a
Christian. Make
sure kids know
when and where
they can ask
questions.

Questions from kids video (3 minutes)

Show the "Unit 20, Session 3" questions from kids video.
Prompt kids to think about John's words to his followers.
Guide them to discuss whether or not it is wrong to want
to be famous. Help them consider how God's glory is more
important than our own.

· "Unit 20, Session 3"
questions from kids
video

Missions moment (3 minutes)

Display the Thiemann family photo and ask for a
volunteer to read the caption.

· "Thiemann Family
Photo" printable

LEADER • The Thiemanns live in LeSotho (leh-SOO-too),
a small country in southern Africa. Jason Thiemann
is a pilot and mechanic with Mission Aviation
Fellowship. Life in LeSotho isn't always easy, but they
are there to be obedient to Jesus and to share the
gospel. John the Baptist told people to follow Jesus.
That's what missionaries do, too.

Key passage (5 minutes)

Show the key passage poster. Lead the boys and girls to read
together John 3:30.

· Key Passage Poster
· "He Must Increase,
but I Must Decrease
(John 3:30)" song

LEADER • John knew that it was his time to fade into the

Prepare the Way

backdrop, but God was not done with him. Even though John was no longer leading a movement, he was paving the way for us to see what it means to follow Jesus. John was put into prison for standing up for the truth. John discovered that decreasing to increase Jesus comes through being willing to give up everything to follow Jesus. Was it hard? Yes. Was it worth it? Definitely. Through our obedience, God plans to bring life and blessing to those around us. We say with John, "I must decrease."

Lead boys and girls in singing "He Must Increase, but I Must Decrease (John 3:30)."

Sing (4 minutes)

Open your Bible and read aloud Acts 4:12.

LEADER • We follow Jesus and no one else because Jesus is the One who brings salvation. When we trust in Him, we are saved from sin and death. Praise God! Let's sing.

Sing together "Take It to the Lord."

Pray (2 minutes)

Invite kids to pray before dismissing to apply the story.

LEADER • God, thank You for sending Your Son. Help us treasure Jesus most of all. Grow our hearts for the nations and give us boldness to share the gospel with others wherever we go. We want to live for Your glory because You are worthy. Amen.

Dismiss to apply the story

· "Take It to the Lord" song
· Bible

The Gospel: God's Plan for Me

Ask kids if they have ever heard the word *gospel*. Clarify that the word *gospel* means "good news." It is the message about Christ, the kingdom of God, and salvation. Use the following guide to share the gospel with kids.

God rules. Explain to kids that the Bible tells us God created everything, and He is in charge of everything. Invite a volunteer to read Genesis 1:1 from the Bible. Read Revelation 4:11 or Colossians 1:16-17 aloud and explain what these verses mean.

We sinned. Tell kids that since the time of Adam and Eve, everyone has chosen to disobey God. (Romans 3:23) The Bible calls this sin. Because God is holy, God cannot be around sin. Sin separates us from God and deserves God's punishment of death. (Romans 6:23)

God provided. Choose a child to read John 3:16 aloud. Say that God sent His Son, Jesus, the perfect solution to our sin problem, to rescue us from the punishment we deserve. It's something we, as sinners, could never earn on our own. Jesus alone saves us. Read and explain Ephesians 2:8-9.

Jesus gives. Share with kids that Jesus lived a perfect life, died on the cross for our sins, and rose again. Because Jesus gave up His life for us, we can be welcomed into God's family for eternity. This is the best gift ever! Read Romans 5:8; 2 Corinthians 5:21; or 1 Peter 3:18.

We respond. Tell kids that they can respond to Jesus. Read Romans 10:9-10,13. Review these aspects of our response: Believe in your heart that Jesus alone saves you through what He's already done on the cross. Repent, turning from self and sin to Jesus. Tell God and others that your faith is in Jesus.

Offer to talk with any child who is interested in responding to Jesus. Provide *I'm a Christian Now!* for new Christians to take home and complete with their families.

APPLY the Story

SESSION TITLE: John Pointed to Jesus

BIBLE PASSAGE: Matthew 3; John 1; 3

STORY POINT: John the Baptist told people to follow Jesus.

KEY PASSAGE: John 3:30

BIG PICTURE QUESTION: Why did Jesus become human? Jesus became human to obey His Father's plan and rescue sinners.

Key passage activity (5 minutes)

· Key Passage Poster
· masking tape
· permanent marker

Write the words of the key passage on separate pieces of masking tape. Prepare one strip per kid—words may be repeated. Tape a word to the toe of each kid's shoe. Instruct kids to stand in a circle (in any order).

Display the key passage poster. Lead them to say the key passage slowly. Each time a kid hears the word on his shoe, he should hop once. Repeat at a faster pace as kids learn the key passage.

SAY • Our key passage comes from our Bible story today. Who said these words? (*John*) To whom was he speaking? (*his followers*)

Allow volunteers who have memorized the key passage to recite it from memory.

Discussion & Bible skills (10 minutes)

· Bibles, 1 per kid
· Story Point Poster

Distribute Bibles. Guide boys and girls to open their Bibles to John 3. Explain the Bible story today is from the Gospel of John, the fourth book in the New Testament. John was one of the 12 men whom Jesus chose to be His disciples. John wrote about the life and words of Jesus. Choose a volunteer to read aloud John 3:35-36.

SAY • *Why did Jesus become human? Jesus became human to obey His Father's plan and rescue sinners.* John's job was to point people to Jesus. John the Baptist told people to get ready for Jesus, the promised Messiah.

Ask the following questions. Lead the group to discuss:

1. Why did John say Jesus must increase and he (John) must decrease? *Prompt kids to recall that with Jesus on earth, John's mission was complete. Jesus was the One whom people had been waiting for—the promised Messiah who would save people from their sins! Jesus was greater than John, and John joyfully stepped aside as Jesus began His earthly ministry.*
   (Option: Choose a volunteer to read Luke 14:11.)

2. Who deserves fame and glory in our own lives—us or God? Why? *Help kids recognize that even when you work hard to accomplish something great, you can give God glory because He made you and gives you special talents and abilities. Prompt them to discuss ways they can make Jesus famous instead of trying to make a great name for themselves.*
   (Option: Choose a volunteer to read Matt. 5:16.)

3. How can we point others to Jesus? *Invite kids to discuss how we can tell people directly about Jesus, and we can also show kindness and have peace in a way that shows we trust Jesus with our lives and our future.*
   (Option: Choose a volunteer to read 1 Pet. 3:15.)

Option: Retell or review the Bible story using the bolded text of the Bible story script.

Activity choice (10 minutes)

OPTION 1: Missions travel kits

Bring an assortment of travel supplies and invite kids to assemble travel kits. Seal the supplies in plastic

· small travel items (toothbrushes, toothpaste, mouthwash, deodorant)
· ziplock bags
· index cards or construction paper
· crayons

Tip: Use this activity option to reinforce the missions moment from Teach the Story.

sandwich bags. Ask kids to include a short note or draw a picture and put one in each bag.

SAY • We will make travel kits for members in our church who are going on mission trips. This is one way we can support their trip even if we can't go ourselves.

Pray for people in your church or others you know who are going on mission trips. Give the bags to your church staff or missions committee to be distributed.

OPTION 2: Mission complete

List on a piece of paper 5 to 10 tasks kids can complete in the classroom. Make two copies of the task list. Sample tasks:

- *Count how many steps it takes to walk from one side of the room to the other.*
- *Tell your leader your favorite movie.*
- *Sing the alphabet song.*
- *Do 20 jumping jacks.*
- *Recite the key passage, John 3:30.*
- *Answer the big picture question:* **Why did Jesus become human?**
- *High-five three other people.*

Form two teams. Provide each team with a prepared task list. Signal teams to begin. Kids should work with their teams to complete the tasks. When a team finishes, its players should sit down and shout, "Mission complete!"

SAY • Finishing something you worked hard at feels great. **John the Baptist told people to follow Jesus.** Now that Jesus was there, John's mission was complete. Jesus was greater than John, and John joyfully stepped aside as Jesus began His earthly ministry.

Because we know that Jesus is good, we can find

LOW PREP

· paper
· marker

Option: Review the gospel with boys and girls. Explain that kids are welcome to speak with you or another teacher if they have questions.

joy in pointing others to Jesus. We don't need fame or recognition for the things we accomplish. God gives us talents and abilities to point people to Him. We give glory to Jesus because He gave His life to rescue us.

Journal and prayer (5 minutes)

Distribute journal pages and pencils. Guide kids to think about and answer the questions listed on the page:

- What does this story teach me about God or the gospel?
- What does the story teach me about myself?
- Are there any commands in this story to obey? How are they for God's glory and my good?
- Are there any promises in this story to remember? How do they help me trust and love God?
- How does this story help me to live on mission better?

As kids journal, invite them to share their ideas. Then pray, acknowledging that Jesus tells the truth about God and His kingdom. Thank God for the gift of salvation, which we can receive when we turn away from our sin and turn to Jesus.

As time allows, lead kids to complete "John or Jesus?" on the activity page. Kids should fill in the blanks with the correct name—*John* or *Jesus*.

· pencils
· Journal Page
· "John or Jesus?" activity page, 1 per kid

Tip: Give parents this week's *Big Picture Cards for Families* to allow families to interact with the biblical content at home.

Unit 20 · Session 4
Jesus Called Disciples

BIBLE PASSAGE:
Matthew 4; 9; Mark 1–3; Luke 5–6

STORY POINT:
Jesus called disciples to follow Him.

KEY PASSAGE:
John 3:30

BIG PICTURE QUESTION:
Why did Jesus become human?
Jesus became human to obey His
Father's plan and rescue sinners.

INTRODUCE THE STORY
(10–15 MINUTES)
PAGE 150

→

TEACH THE STORY
(25–30 MINUTES)
PAGE 152

→

APPLY THE STORY
(25–30 MINUTES)
PAGE 158

Additional resources are available at gospelproject.com. For free training and session-by-session help, visit ministrygrid.com/gospelproject.

LEADER Bible Study

In the first century, *rabbi* was a title given to a respected expert in the law of Moses. A rabbi studied the Scriptures and taught through speaking and writing. Jews wanted to honor God in how they lived, and they looked to the rabbis to instruct them in their behavior.

The word *rabbi* translates "my master." Jewish students would seek out a rabbi and ask to follow him. A rabbi would choose only a few highly-promising students to be his disciples. If a student was not accepted by the rabbi, he likely returned home to learn a trade. Those chosen to be a rabbi's disciples followed him everywhere. They learned from the rabbi how to think and how to act. They trusted the rabbi, and the goal was to become just like him.

When Jesus chose His disciples, His strategy was unusual. Rather than waiting for students to come to Him, Jesus sought out His disciples among the people who followed Him. He found them working—fishing and repairing nets. Some of Jesus' disciples were introduced to Him by their friends. He approached these ordinary men and said, "Follow Me." Their response? "Immediately they left ... and followed him" (Matt. 4:20,22).

The Twelve—Simon (Peter) and his brother Andrew; James and John; Philip; Bartholomew; Matthew; Thomas; James, son of Alphaeus; Thaddaeus; Simon; and Judas—spent time with Jesus during His ministry. Jesus taught them how to live in light of God's coming kingdom. He commissioned them to teach others about Him. The good news about Jesus is too great to not share with the entire world.

The call to follow Jesus is not an easy one. Jesus said, "If anyone wants to follow after me, let him deny himself, take up his cross, and follow me" (Matt. 16:24). Jesus calls us to do the same—to surrender our lives for His purposes and perhaps even to die. "For whoever wants to save his life will lose it, but whoever loses his life because of me will find it" (Matt. 16:25).

4

Prepare the Way

The **BIBLE** Story

Jesus Called Disciples
Matthew 4; 9; Mark 1–3; Luke 5–6

Jesus' ministry had begun. He traveled around, preaching about God and telling people to turn away from their sins. People started talking about Jesus and the things He was teaching. They were interested in what Jesus had to say. **Large crowds followed Jesus around and listened to Him teach.**

One day, Jesus was walking along the Sea of Galilee. He saw two brothers: Simon—who was called Peter—and Andrew. Peter and Andrew were fishermen. **Jesus called out to them, "Follow Me, and I will teach you to fish for people!" Right away, Peter and Andrew dropped their nets and followed Jesus.**

Later, He saw two more brothers. Their names were James and John. They were in a boat fixing nets with their father, Zebedee. **Jesus called out to them, and right away they got up, left their father and the boat, and followed Jesus.**

Jesus went on and saw a man named Matthew (who was also called Levi). Matthew was sitting at the tax office. Matthew was a tax collector. Many people didn't like tax collectors because tax collectors were unfair. **Jesus called out to him, "Follow Me!" So Matthew got up, left everything behind, and**

followed Jesus.

Matthew had a big feast for Jesus at his house. Many tax collectors and sinners came to eat with Jesus and His disciples. The religious leaders saw this, and they didn't think Jesus should be friends with people who did wrong things. They complained to the disciples, "Why does your Teacher eat and drink with tax collectors and sinners?"

Jesus heard the religious leaders and said, "People who are healthy don't need a doctor, but people who are sick do. I did not come to invite good people; I came to invite sinners to turn back to God."

Later, Jesus gathered His followers together and chose twelve of them to be His apostles. Jesus' apostles would work closely with Jesus and would go out to tell others about Him. These are the men Jesus chose: Simon (who was called Peter), Simon's brother Andrew, James and John (who were called the "Sons of Thunder"), Philip and Bartholomew, Matthew and Thomas, James the son of Alphaeus (al FEE uhs), Thaddaeus (THAD ih uhs), Simon the Zealot, and Judas Iscariot (iss KAR ih aht).

Christ Connection: Jesus came to earth to show what God is like and to save people from their sins. This is great news! Jesus told His disciples to tell others about Him, and we are Jesus' disciples when we trust in Him. Everyone in the world needs to hear the good news about Jesus.

Bible Storytelling Tips

- **List names:** Write the disciples' names on a dry erase board and point to them as you tell the story.
- **Use props:** Display fishing nets as you tell about the fishermen who left their nets to follow Jesus.

INTRODUCE the Story

SESSION TITLE: Jesus Called Disciples
BIBLE PASSAGE: Matthew 4; 9; Mark 1–3; Luke 5–6
STORY POINT: Jesus called disciples to follow Him.
KEY PASSAGE: John 3:30
BIG PICTURE QUESTION: Why did Jesus become human? Jesus became human to obey His Father's plan and rescue sinners.

Welcome time

Greet each kid as he or she arrives. Use this time to collect the offering, fill out attendance sheets, and help new kids connect to your group. Prompt kids to share about one or two of their closest friends. How long have they known each other? How did they meet?

Activity page (5 minutes)

- "The Twelve" activity page, 1 per kid
- pencils or markers

Invite kids to complete "The Twelve" on the activity page. Guide kids to find and circle the names of Jesus' disciples. Point out that two of the disciples were named James, so the name *James* appears twice in the word search.

SAY • When Jesus began His ministry, many people followed Him and learned from His teaching. We will see in today's Bible story that Jesus chose 12 people to be His disciples. *Disciple* means "learner" or "student."

Session starter (10 minutes)

LOW PREP

OPTION 1: Find a friend
Instruct kids to stand and spread out around the room. Explain that you will call out a description, and kids will

form groups accordingly. Give an example: Find a friend whose birthday is in the same month as yours. Kids should quickly move to stand next to kids who share a birthday month. Groups may consist of more than two kids. Call out additional descriptions as time allows. Consider using the following descriptions: Find a friend who ...

- has the same number of siblings as you
- has the same number of letters in his or her name
- has the same favorite color
- is wearing the same color of shirt

SAY • You formed groups based on specific qualifications. If you had to form of group of people you were going to hang out with all the time, what kind of people would you choose? Today we will hear about the people Jesus chose to be His followers. They weren't famous or powerful. Let's find out more.

Tip: If a kid is unable to find a friend who fits the description, call out his requirement ("four siblings," for example) to make sure there is no match and then move on to the next description.

OPTION 2: Disciples concentration

Form groups of two to six kids. Give each group two copies of the "Disciple Cards." One player in the group should mix up the cards facedown and arrange them in a grid.

· "Disciple Cards" printable

Players will take turns flipping over two cards at a time, trying to find a match. If the cards match, the player collects them. If the cards do not match, the player should turn them facedown again. Play passes to the next kid. The player to collect the most matches wins.

SAY • These cards tell us about Jesus' twelve disciples. **Jesus called disciples to follow Him.** Today we will learn more about who these disciples were and how they responded to Jesus' call, "Follow Me!"

Transition to teach the story

TEACH the Story

SESSION TITLE: Jesus Called Disciples
BIBLE PASSAGE: Matthew 4; 9; Mark 1–3; Luke 5–6
STORY POINT: Jesus called disciples to follow Him.
KEY PASSAGE: John 3:30
BIG PICTURE QUESTION: Why did Jesus become human? Jesus became human to obey His Father's plan and rescue sinners.

Countdown

· countdown video

Show the countdown video as you transition to teach the story. Set it to end as the session begins.

Introduce the session (3 minutes)

· leader attire
· stop sign
· message board
· Bibles

[Leader enters wearing khaki pants, a reflective shirt or vest, and a hard hat. Leader carries a stop sign made from poster board attached to a tall broomstick. A traffic message board reads FOLLOW DETOURS.*]*

Tip: If you prefer not to use themed content or characters, adapt or omit this introduction.

LEADER • You're back! I'm so glad you've come. This road work is nearly complete and I was a little worried I might miss you. We have a portion of the road closed for paving and set up a detour, so a lot of drivers have been finding alternate routes and avoiding the area altogether. You'd be surprised, though, how many people insist on going around the traffic barriers to take their normal route. I tell them that's not a good idea. When there's a detour, you can't ignore it; you have to follow it! Otherwise you could find yourself in a pretty dangerous situation.

Say, did you bring your Bibles today? *[Encourage kids to hold up their Bibles, or distribute Bibles.]* I have one more story to share with you. It's about a time when Jesus called a group of people to follow Him. Let's find out what happened.

Big picture question (1 minute)

LEADER • First, keep our big picture question and answer in mind. *Why did Jesus become human? Jesus became human to obey His Father's plan and rescue sinners.* Each time you hear a story about Jesus and wonder, *why did He do that?* I want you to remember this question and answer. Everything Jesus did on earth was according to God's perfect plan.

Giant timeline (1 minute)

Show the giant timeline. Point to individual Bible stories as you review.

· Giant Timeline

LEADER • Look at our timeline. When Jesus came on the scene as an adult, He went to John to be baptized. **Jesus obeyed God by being baptized.** Then Jesus was tempted by the Devil in the wilderness. **Jesus was tempted and never sinned.** Soon, John's followers started asking questions about Jesus, and **John the Baptist told people to follow Jesus.**

Today's Bible story is about a special group of people Jesus called to follow Him. They were His twelve disciples. Check this out.

Tell the Bible story (10 minutes)

Open your Bible to Matthew 4; 9; Mark 1–3; Luke 5–6. Use the Bible storytelling tips on the Bible story page to help you tell the story, or show the Bible story video "Jesus Called Disciples."

· Bibles
· "Jesus Called Disciples" video
· Big Picture Question Poster
· Bible Story Picture Poster
· Story Point Poster

LEADER • The disciples were busy when Jesus showed up. **Jesus called disciples to follow Him**, and isn't it amazing that they immediately left what they were doing and followed Him? They didn't say, "We will follow You, just let us finish up here," or "Let me work through the end of the month and then I'll follow You." What did they do? Look at Mark 1:18. [*Allow kid to read the verse and respond.*] Two brothers even left their dad behind. [*See Mark 1:19-20.*] I wonder what their dad thought about that!

In those days, only the best students approached teachers and asked to follow them. The students watched their teachers very carefully. They tried to be just like the teachers. Teachers didn't allow just anyone to follow them; you had to be a very hard worker, and the teacher had to think you were pretty special too.

Jesus chose His followers from a group of people no one probably ever thought was smart enough to be students. Jesus' followers were called disciples. Jesus chose some fishermen: Peter, Andrew, James, and John. Then He chose a tax collector named Matthew. The other men Jesus chose were Philip, Bartholomew, Thomas, James, Thaddaeus, Simon, and Judas. Yes, two of Jesus' twelve disciples were named James! Jesus' disciples would learn from Jesus so that they could tell others the good news about why Jesus came: to save people from their sins.

Christ connection

LEADER • Jesus came to earth to show what God is like and to save people from their sins. This is great news!

Tip: Use Scripture and the guide provided on page 157 to explain how to become a Christian. Make sure kids know when and where they can ask questions.

Jesus told His disciples to tell others about Him, and we are Jesus' disciples when we trust in Him. Everyone in the world needs to hear the good news about Jesus.

Questions from kids video (3 minutes)

Show the "Unit 20, Session 4" questions from kids video. Prompt kids to think about their own plans and hopes for the future. Guide them to discuss whether it is easy or hard to trust God's plan.

- "Unit 20, Session 4" questions from kids video

Missions moment (3 minutes)

Give each kid a copy of the "How Kids Can Help MAF" printable.

Ask for volunteers to read aloud some of the ways that kids can get involved in helping a mission organization like Mission Aviation Fellowship. Specifically look at the prayer list on page 2. Take time together to pray for some of the requests. Direct kids to keep the printable for a later activity or to take home.

- "How Kids Can Help MAF" printable

LEADER • Our prayers for missionaries are very important and it's important for us to remember that we can be on mission wherever we go. **Jesus called disciples to follow Him.** We are Jesus' disciples when we trust in Him. Everyone in the world needs to hear the good news about Jesus.

Key passage (5 minutes)

Show the key passage poster. Lead the boys and girls to read together John 3:30.

LEADER • What if we don't decrease in order to increase Jesus' fame and worth? Is this optional or only for

- Key Passage Poster
- "He Must Increase, but I Must Decrease (John 3:30)" song

certain Christians? No, this is the path of all of God's people. Following Jesus can be hard. As we love people and they come to know Jesus, they might be tempted to follow us instead of Jesus. Our key passage creates in us humility that keeps us, like John, pointing everyone to Jesus and away from ourselves as the answer to all of life's problems. Let's sing together.

Lead boys and girls in singing "He Must Increase, but I Must Decrease (John 3:30)."

Sing (4 minutes)

- "Take It to the Lord" song
- Bible

Open your Bible and read aloud Psalm 118:28-29.

LEADER • Think about this: God the Son came down to earth to be with us. *Why did Jesus become human? Jesus became human to obey His Father's plan and rescue sinners.* He calls us to follow Him. He is faithful and good. Let's sing.

Sing together "Take It to the Lord."

Pray (2 minutes)

Invite kids to pray before dismissing to apply the story.

LEADER • God, thank You for sending Jesus to save us from our sin. We pray You would work in the hearts of those who don't know You to repent and become followers of Jesus—trusting Him, obeying Him, and telling others about Him. We want to be faithful followers. We need You. Amen.

Dismiss to apply the story

The Gospel: God's Plan for Me

Ask kids if they have ever heard the word *gospel*. Clarify that the word *gospel* means "good news." It is the message about Christ, the kingdom of God, and salvation. Use the following guide to share the gospel with kids.

God rules. Explain to kids that the Bible tells us God created everything, and He is in charge of everything. Invite a volunteer to read Genesis 1:1 from the Bible. Read Revelation 4:11 or Colossians 1:16-17 aloud and explain what these verses mean.

We sinned. Tell kids that since the time of Adam and Eve, everyone has chosen to disobey God. (Romans 3:23) The Bible calls this sin. Because God is holy, God cannot be around sin. Sin separates us from God and deserves God's punishment of death. (Romans 6:23)

God provided. Choose a child to read John 3:16 aloud. Say that God sent His Son, Jesus, the perfect solution to our sin problem, to rescue us from the punishment we deserve. It's something we, as sinners, could never earn on our own. Jesus alone saves us. Read and explain Ephesians 2:8-9.

Jesus gives. Share with kids that Jesus lived a perfect life, died on the cross for our sins, and rose again. Because Jesus gave up His life for us, we can be welcomed into God's family for eternity. This is the best gift ever! Read Romans 5:8; 2 Corinthians 5:21; or 1 Peter 3:18.

We respond. Tell kids that they can respond to Jesus. Read Romans 10:9-10,13. Review these aspects of our response: Believe in your heart that Jesus alone saves you through what He's already done on the cross. Repent, turning from self and sin to Jesus. Tell God and others that your faith is in Jesus.

Offer to talk with any child who is interested in responding to Jesus. Provide *I'm a Christian Now!* for new Christians to take home and complete with their families.

APPLY the Story

SESSION TITLE: Jesus Called Disciples

BIBLE PASSAGE: Matthew 4; 9; Mark 1–3; Luke 5–6

STORY POINT: Jesus called disciples to follow Him.

KEY PASSAGE: John 3:30

BIG PICTURE QUESTION: Why did Jesus become human? Jesus became human to obey His Father's plan and rescue sinners.

Key passage activity (5 minutes)

- Key Passage Poster
- clothespins or strips of paper
- fine-point marker

Before the session, write each word of the key passage—including the reference—on a separate clothespin or strip of paper. Prepare two sets.

Display the key passage poster. Lead kids in reading aloud John 3:30 together.

Form two teams. Mix up each team's clothespins and pile them at one side of the room. Instruct teams to line up at the other side of the room. Explain that when you say "go," the first player on each team will run to the pile, grab the clothespin with the first word of the key passage, and then return to her team. Then the second player will retrieve the second word, and so on until a team collects all of its clothespins in order.

If a clothespin is retrieved out of order, a player must return it and pick up the correct word. When a team finishes, players should sit down. Lead both teams to say the key passage together.

SAY • Great job. Who must increase? (*Jesus*) Who must decrease? (*John*) Like John, we must decrease too! Jesus calls all believers to go and make disciples. We point others not to ourselves but to Jesus!

Discussion & Bible skills (10 minutes)

Distribute Bibles. Guide boys and girls to open their Bibles to Matthew 4. Explain that today's Bible story is found in three of the four Gospels—Matthew; Mark; and Luke. Jesus was walking along the Sea of Galilee when He called His disciples. [*Point to the Sea of Galilee (D6) on the New Testament Israel Map.*] Choose a volunteer to read aloud Matthew 4:19-20.

SAY • Jesus told the men He called that He would teach them to fish for people. But they wouldn't use nets or boats; they would use their words to gather people and tell them about Jesus.

Ask the following questions. Lead the group to discuss:

1. Why do you think Jesus picked fishermen and tax collectors to be His disciples instead of kings or religious leaders? *Invite kids to share their ideas. Share that the Bible says God uses people who have nothing to offer to show His power and strength through them.* (Option: Choose a volunteer to read 1 Cor. 1:26-31.)

2. What does it mean to follow Jesus? *Prompt kids to recognize that following Jesus means trusting Him, obeying Him, and telling others about Him.* (Option: Choose a volunteer to read Matt. 16:24.)

3. What do you think might keep someone from following Jesus? *Help kids understand that everyone follows something, and we follow what we value the most. Some people live for family and friends, for themselves, for popularity, or for money. The Bible says we must follow Jesus and nothing else. We can pray that God will soften the hearts of those who do not follow Jesus so that they would come to know and love Him.* (Option: Choose a volunteer to read 1 Cor. 1:18.)

· Bibles, 1 per kid
· Story Point Poster
· Small Group Timeline and Map Set
(005802970)

Option: Retell or review the Bible story using the bolded text of the Bible story script.

Prepare the Way

LOW PREP

- "How Kids Can Help MAF" printable
- crayons

Tip: Use this activity option to reinforce the missions moment from Teach the Story.

- Gospel Plan Poster
- markers
- index cards
- Bibles

Option: Review the gospel with boys and girls. Explain that kids are welcome to speak with you or another teacher if they have questions.

Activity choice (10 minutes)

OPTION 1: Explore missions

Provide copies of the "How Kids Can Help MAF" printable. Kids may already have the printable from the missions moment. Allow time for kids to color the handout and complete the activities. Ask kids questions about the airplane they like the best or where they might like to fly one day. Listen for interest in a future mission project to help support MAF or other missionaries.

SAY • When we learn about missionaries and how to support them, we are part of God's plan to reach all people with the gospel. No matter your age, you can be on mission!

OPTION 2: God's plan for us

Use the gospel plan poster to present the gospel to kids. Give each kid a marker and five index cards. Provide copies of the gospel plan poster for kids to reference. Invite kids to draw the gospel plan logos on separate cards and caption the logos. (*crown: God rules; X: we sinned; cross: God provided; present: Jesus gives; hands: we respond*)

Encourage kids to form pairs and practice sharing the gospel, using the icons as prompts. Kids may also read the referenced Bible verses. Suggest kids continue practicing throughout the week to become more comfortable with sharing the gospel.

SAY • *Why did Jesus become human? Jesus became human to obey His Father's plan and rescue sinners.* He showed people what God is like. When He began His ministry, **Jesus called disciples to follow Him.**

Jesus told His disciples to tell others about Him, and we are Jesus' disciples when we trust in Him.

Everyone in the world needs to hear the good news about Jesus. The gospel is the good news: the message about Jesus, the kingdom of God, and salvation. You can use these five pictures—drawn on a notebook, on a napkin, in the dirt, or anywhere else—to explain the good news to others.

Journal and prayer (5 minutes)

Distribute journal pages and pencils. Guide kids to think about and answer the questions listed on the page:

- What does this story teach me about God or the gospel?
- What does the story teach me about myself?
- Are there any commands in this story to obey? How are they for God's glory and my good?
- Are there any promises in this story to remember? How do they help me trust and love God?
- How does this story help me to live on mission better?

As kids journal, invite them to share their ideas. Then pray, praising God for coming to earth to be with us. Thank God for not leaving us dead in our sin but for rescuing us and calling us to join His work in sharing the gospel with the whole world. Pray that kids who have not yet responded to Jesus' call would follow Him.

As time allows, lead kids to complete "Connection Point" on the activity page. Kids should decode the messages. (Hint: 1 = A, 2 = B, 3 = C ...).

· pencils
· Journal Page
· "Connection Point" activity page, 1 per kid

Tip: Give parents this week's *Big Picture Cards for Families* to allow families to interact with the biblical content at home.

Use Week of:

Unit 21 · Session 1
Jesus' Early Miracles

BIBLE PASSAGE:
Mark 1

STORY POINT:
People came to Jesus, and
He healed them.

KEY PASSAGE:
John 3:16

BIG PICTURE QUESTION:
What makes people special?
People are special because we are
made in God's image, as male and
female, to know Him.

INTRODUCE THE STORY (10–15 MINUTES) PAGE 166	TEACH THE STORY (25–30 MINUTES) PAGE 168	APPLY THE STORY (25–30 MINUTES) PAGE 174

Additional resources are available at gospelproject.com. For free training and session-by-session help, visit ministrygrid.com/gospelproject.

LEADER Bible Study

Early in His ministry, Jesus and His disciples traveled to Capernaum, a town on the northwestern shore of the Sea of Galilee. Capernaum became Jesus' home and headquarters. (See Matt. 4:13.) He entered the synagogue on the Sabbath, when people would gather to hear and learn from the Scriptures.

Jesus quickly set Himself apart from the scribes and other religious teachers. Unlike the scribes, who relied completely on traditional interpretations of the Torah from other teachers, Jesus spoke with authority. His teaching came from His own authority as the Author of truth, and it had a profound effect on His listeners—they were astonished!

The early miracles recorded in Mark 1 demonstrate Jesus' power and authority as the Son of God. Jesus drove an unclean spirit from a man in the synagogue; even the demons obey His commands. Then Jesus healed Peter's mother-in-law, and that evening the people in the town brought to Jesus all those who were sick or afflicted with unclean spirits. What did Jesus do? He healed them! (Mark 1:34)

Jesus' miracles continued, and He healed a man with leprosy. *Leprosy* is a skin disease that would have marked a person as "unclean," requiring him to be separated from the community. Jesus had compassion on the man and healed him immediately.

Jesus' miracles brought many people to faith in Him. They also proved that Jesus is the Messiah, the Son of God. These miracles strengthened people's faith and met their needs. Isaiah prophesied that the promised Messiah would bear our sickness and carry our pain. (Isa. 53:4) Jesus fulfilled this prophecy as He healed people.

Help kids make the connection that through Jesus, God did what is impossible for us to do on our own. He provided forgiveness, salvation, and eternal life for all who would trust in Him.

The **BIBLE** Story

Jesus' Early Miracles
Mark 1

Jesus traveled to Capernaum (kuh PUHR nay uhm) with His disciples Simon, Andrew, James, and John. He **went into the synagogue on the Sabbath and began to teach. The people there were very surprised. Jesus' teaching was not like the scribes' teaching. He spoke with authority.**

Just then, a man with an unclean spirit shouted, "What do You have to do with us, Jesus of Nazareth? Have You come to destroy us? **I know who You are—the Holy One of God!" Jesus commanded the spirit to be quiet and come out of the man. The spirit yelled again and then came out.**

Everyone was amazed! **"Who is this Jesus?" they asked. "He teaches with authority, and the unclean spirits obey Him!"** News about Jesus spread quickly throughout all of Galilee.

Next, Jesus and His disciples went to Simon and Andrew's house. Simon's mother-in-law was in bed with a fever. Jesus went to her, took her hand, and healed her. She got up and began to serve them. **That evening, large crowds of people came to the house with others who were sick or bothered by evil spirits, and Jesus healed them.**

Early the next morning, Jesus went out by Himself to pray. Simon and the other disciples found Him and said, "Everyone is looking for You."

Jesus said, "Let's go on to the nearby villages so I can preach there too. This is why I have come."

Jesus traveled throughout Galilee. He preached and drove out demons. A man with a skin disease came to Jesus. He got on his knees and begged: "If You are willing, You can make me clean." Jesus was willing, and He healed the man.

Christ Connection: Jesus' miracles proved that Jesus is the Messiah, the Son of God. They strengthened people's faith and met their needs. Through Jesus, God did what is impossible for us to do on our own. He provided forgiveness, salvation, and eternal life.

Bible Storytelling Tips

• **Change pace:** Draw attention to dialogue by slowing your pace slightly when speaking dialogue.
• **Pause for effect:** Use pauses and silence between paragraphs to capture kids' attention.

INTRODUCE the Story

SESSION TITLE: Jesus' Early Miracles

BIBLE PASSAGE: Mark 1

STORY POINT: People came to Jesus, and He healed them.

KEY PASSAGE: John 3:16

BIG PICTURE QUESTION: What makes people special? People are special because we are made in God's image, as male and female, to know Him.

Welcome time

Greet each kid as he or she arrives. Use this time to collect the offering, fill out attendance sheets, and help new kids connect to your group. Prompt kids to share about a time someone helped them do something this week. Kids may also share about ways they have helped others. Lead them to consider why people help one another.

Activity page (5 minutes)

- "Story Tangle" activity page, 1 per kid
- pencils or markers

Invite kids to complete "Story Tangle" on the activity page. Kids should follow the lines to put the letters in the blanks.

SAY • What word did you discover? (*healed*) **People came to Jesus, and He healed them.** That is amazing. The Bible tells us about many miracles Jesus performed while He was on earth. Today we will hear about some of the miracles Jesus did early in His ministry, and—more importantly—why He did them.

Session starter (10 minutes)

OPTION 1: Are you willing?

Tell kids that you need a volunteer. Call a kid with his hand raised to stand at the front of the class. Explain his task and then ask, "Are you willing to do that?" If he is not, let him sit back down. If he is, give him the opportunity to complete the task. Repeat with new volunteers for each additional task. Sample tasks:

- Sing the happy birthday song.
- Give everyone a high-five.
- Pretend you are a cat for the rest of the game.
- Do 10 jumping jacks.
- Show us your best dance moves.
- Pretend that you are underwater for 30 seconds.

SAY • In today's Bible story, a man believed Jesus could help him if Jesus was willing. Do you think He was? Let's find out.

OPTION 2: Miracle matches

Print three sets of the "Miracles of Jesus Game" printable on colored paper. Wad the statements into small balls and scatter them over the floor.

- watch or timer
- "Miracles of Jesus Game" printable
- colored paper

Form two teams. Explain that the paper wads describe eight miracles Jesus performed. The kids' task is to match the miracles. Each miracle has three statements. One team will play at a time. Give a team's players 30 seconds to open the papers. If a team finds all three of the matches, the team earns one point. When time is up, instruct players to wad up the statements and return them all to the floor.

Play multiple rounds until kids find the sets for eight miracles.

SAY • The Bible records dozens of miracles Jesus performed. Today we will hear about some of the miracles Jesus performed early in His ministry.

Transition to teach the story

TEACH the Story

SESSION TITLE: Jesus' Early Miracles

BIBLE PASSAGE: Mark 1

STORY POINT: People came to Jesus, and He healed them.

KEY PASSAGE: John 3:16

BIG PICTURE QUESTION: What makes people special? People are special because we are made in God's image, as male and female, to know Him.

· room decorations
· Theme Background Slide (optional)

Suggested Theme Decorating Ideas: Simulate an ambulance bay. Attach a large square of foam board to a focal wall. Decorate the square to look like the rear doors of an ambulance. Include windows, lights, and a bumper. Position a small shelf or open cabinet to one side and fill it with first aid supplies. Display a stretcher or backboard, if available, or drape a sheet over a table to act as a stretcher. You may also choose to project the theme background slide

Countdown

· countdown video

Show the countdown video as you transition to teach the story. Set it to end as the session begins.

Introduce the session (3 minutes)

· leader attire
· disposable gloves
· stethoscope
· Bible

Tip: If you prefer not to use themed content or characters, adapt or omit this introduction.

[Leader enters wearing dark pants, a solid-color shirt, disposable gloves, and a stethoscope.]

LEADER • Hello! Thank you for coming today. I'm [*your name*], a paramedic. Does anyone know what a paramedic does? [*Allow kids to respond.*] Paramedics are healthcare professionals who are trained to respond to emergency medical calls outside the hospital. If you're in a life-threatening situation and call 911, paramedics can come straight to you with some of the same services you can find in an emergency room.

Encountering so many people in order to help them is really rewarding, but this can be a tough job. It makes me look forward even more to the day when there will be no more pain and suffering.

When Jesus encountered people on earth, He changed their lives in extraordinary ways. Let me tell you about it.

Big picture question (1 minute)

LEADER • As you hear today's Bible story and the stories for the next few weeks, think about our big picture question. This question helps us remember that God is doing something bigger beyond the specific events of the story.

The question is, *What makes people special?* This is a great question. Jesus spent a lot of His time on earth with people. Here is the answer: *People are special because we are made in God's image, as male and female, to know Him.*

Giant timeline (1 minute)

Show the giant timeline. Point to individual Bible stories as you review.

· Giant Timeline

LEADER • Jesus came to earth as *Immanuel,* which means "God is with us." Jesus began His ministry when He was about thirty years old (Luke 3:23). He called disciples to follow Him and spent much of His time with people. We'll find out today how Jesus changed the lives of many people through His early miracles.

Among the People

- Bibles
- "Jesus' Early
  Miracles" video
- Big Picture Question
  Poster
- Bible Story Picture
  Poster
- Story Point Poster

Tell the Bible story (10 minutes)

Open your Bible to Mark 1. Use the Bible storytelling tips on the Bible story page to help you tell the story, or show the Bible story video "Jesus' Early Miracles."

LEADER • Jesus was at the synagogue in Capernaum. Who else was there? (*Jesus' disciples and other Jews*)

A man with an unclean spirit shouted out. What did the unclean spirit know about Jesus? Look at Mark 1:23-24. [*Allow kids to read the verse and respond.*] Jesus is the Holy One of God. Unclean spirits were quick to recognize Jesus as the Son of God. Jesus commanded the unclean spirit to come out of the man, and the spirit obeyed Him.

Why was the crowd amazed at Jesus? Look at Mark 1:27. [*Allow kids to read the verse and respond.*] Jesus wasn't like other teachers, who taught things they had learned from others. Jesus taught with authority. He even had authority over unclean spirits.

News about Jesus spread throughout the area. **People came to Jesus, and He healed them.** They brought their friends and family members who were sick, and Jesus healed them all.

Jesus' early miracles showed His power and authority as the Son of God.

Christ connection

LEADER • Jesus' miracles proved that Jesus is the Messiah, the Son of God. They strengthened people's faith and met their needs. *What makes people special? People are special because we are made in God's image, as male and female, to know Him.*

Through Jesus, God did what is impossible for

Tip: Use Scripture and the guide provided on page 173 to explain how to become a Christian. Make sure kids know when and where they can ask questions.

Older Kids Leader Guide
Unit 21 • Session 1

us to do on our own. He provided forgiveness, salvation, and eternal life.

Questions from kids video (3 minutes)

Show the "Unit 21, Session 1" questions from kids video. Prompt kids to think about God's ability to perform miracles. Guide them to discuss evidence they can recognize as proof that God is still at work in the world today.

· "Unit 21, Session 1" questions from kids video

Missions moment (3 minutes)

Ask kids if they know how sports can be used in missions. Some will remember previous mission stories involving sports evangelism.

· "Better Than Basketball" missions video

LEADER • Every sport you play and every hobby you enjoy can be used to share the love of Jesus. In the Bible, we read that **people came to Jesus, and He healed them.** Jesus heals people today, too, by forgiving their sins and offering eternal life. Let's watch how a basketball player is sharing that message with people in Nevada.

Play the "Better Than Basketball" missions video. Then pray for Heiden Ratner, who is sharing the gospel.

Key passage (5 minutes)

Show the key passage poster. Lead the boys and girls to read together John 3:16.

· Key Passage Poster
· "In This Way" song

LEADER • God is love. He loves the world he created. *What makes people special? People are special because we are made in God's image, as male and female, to know Him.* Yet the unbelieving world does not love God. The world is an enemy of God and fights against His rule and reign. Since sin entered the world, the world has believed the lie that God is not good and loving. This is a lie from Satan.

God is so good that He loves His enemies. His love compelled Him to send Jesus into the world. Let's sing our key passage song to help us remember these words.

Lead boys and girls in singing "In This Way (John 3:16)."

Sing (4 minutes)

Open your Bible and read aloud Psalm 95:1-2.

LEADER • We can show we are thankful to God by singing to Him. Let's sing a song of praise together.

Sing together "Take It to the Lord."

Pray (2 minutes)

Invite kids to pray before dismissing to apply the story.

LEADER • Lord God, as we learn more about You, we are amazed at all You are. No one is like You. The unclean spirits obey You. You have power over sickness and You want to help us! Give us faith to trust that You will give us everything we need. Thank You for forgiveness, salvation, and eternal life. We love You. Amen.

Dismiss to apply the story

- "Take It to the Lord" song
- Bible

The Gospel: God's Plan for Me

Ask kids if they have ever heard the word *gospel*. Clarify that the word *gospel* means "good news." It is the message about Christ, the kingdom of God, and salvation. Use the following guide to share the gospel with kids.

God rules. Explain to kids that the Bible tells us God created everything, and He is in charge of everything. Invite a volunteer to read Genesis 1:1 from the Bible. Read Revelation 4:11 or Colossians 1:16-17 aloud and explain what these verses mean.

We sinned. Tell kids that since the time of Adam and Eve, everyone has chosen to disobey God. (Romans 3:23) The Bible calls this sin. Because God is holy, God cannot be around sin. Sin separates us from God and deserves God's punishment of death. (Romans 6:23)

God provided. Choose a child to read John 3:16 aloud. Say that God sent His Son, Jesus, the perfect solution to our sin problem, to rescue us from the punishment we deserve. It's something we, as sinners, could never earn on our own. Jesus alone saves us. Read and explain Ephesians 2:8-9.

Jesus gives. Share with kids that Jesus lived a perfect life, died on the cross for our sins, and rose again. Because Jesus gave up His life for us, we can be welcomed into God's family for eternity. This is the best gift ever! Read Romans 5:8; 2 Corinthians 5:21; or 1 Peter 3:18.

We respond. Tell kids that they can respond to Jesus. Read Romans 10:9-10,13. Review these aspects of our response: Believe in your heart that Jesus alone saves you through what He's already done on the cross. Repent, turning from self and sin to Jesus. Tell God and others that your faith is in Jesus.

Offer to talk with any child who is interested in responding to Jesus. Provide *I'm a Christian Now!* for new Christians to take home and complete with their families.

Among the People

APPLY the Story

SESSION TITLE: Jesus' Early Miracles

BIBLE PASSAGE: Mark 1

STORY POINT: People came to Jesus, and He healed them.

KEY PASSAGE: John 3:16

BIG PICTURE QUESTION: What makes people special? People are special because we are made in God's image, as male and female, to know Him.

Key passage activity (5 minutes)

· Key Passage Poster
· paper
· crayons or markers

Display the key passage poster. Lead kids in reading aloud John 3:16 together. Give each kid a piece of paper and some crayons. Assign key words or phrases from the passage for kids to illustrate. (Examples: *God, loved, world, gave, Son, everyone, eternal life*) Multiple kids may illustrate the same word. Then lead kids in saying the key passage again, holding up their pictures for the key words.

SAY • John 3:16 tells us the good news of the gospel in one sentence! Work on memorizing our key passage this week. Memorizing God's Word helps us remember what is true. Next week we will see if you can say it from memory.

Discussion & Bible skills (10 minutes)

· Bibles, 1 per kid
· Story Point Poster
· Small Group Timeline and Map Set
  (005802970)

Distribute Bibles. Guide boys and girls to open their Bibles to Mark 1. Explain that the Gospel of Mark tells stories about things Jesus did—healing people, casting out demons, commanding the wind and the waves—to show that Jesus is the Son of God. Choose a volunteer to read aloud Mark 1:40-42.

SAY • Jesus traveled all over Galilee. He taught in

synagogues and told people the good news about God's kingdom. **People came to Jesus, and He healed them.** Large crowds of people followed Jesus around—from Capernaum in Galilee [*point to Capernaum (C6) on the New Testament Israel Map*] to Jerusalem (H4) to Judea (J3) and across the Jordan River (G6).

Ask the following questions. Lead the group to discuss:

Option: Retell or review the Bible story using the bolded text of the Bible story script.

1. How did Jesus' miracles show His care for creation? *Guide kids to discuss how Jesus' miracles restored parts of creation that were affected by sin coming into the world. Jesus cast out unclean spirits, made sick people well, and healed skin diseases. Explain that later in His ministry, Jesus also raised people from the dead, gave sight to people who were blind, and ultimately brought the greatest healing—forgiveness of sins—through His death and resurrection.*
   (Option: Choose a volunteer to read Ps. 77:14.)

2. Do we need to see miracles to believe in Jesus? Why or why not? *Point out that many people saw Jesus' miracles and believed, but Jesus said those who do not see and still believe are blessed. The Bible tells us everything we need to believe in Jesus.*
   (Option: Choose a volunteer to read John 20:29-31.)

3. In what ways does God reveal Himself today? *Lead kids to recognize that God shows us what He is like through the Word—the Bible. The Bible says we can also understand what God is like by looking at His creation. Invite kids to share observations of creation that tell them something about what God is like.*
   (Option: Choose a volunteer to read Rom. 1:19-20.)

Activity choice (10 minutes)

- "On Mission Statements" printable
- basketball or inflatable beach ball
- whistle (optional)

OPTION 1: On mission

Cut out each statement and tape it to a ball. Invite kids to stand in a circle and toss the ball to one another. When you blow the whistle or yell "stop" ask the person holding the ball to complete the statement facing him. If you prefer, let the player choose the statement he wants to answer. Continue play as time allows.

Tip: Use this activity option to reinforce the missions moment from Teach the Story.

SAY • Each of us can be part of God's mission to reach the world with the message of Jesus. Some missionaries, like Heiden Ratner in Nevada, use basketball or other sports to bring people to Jesus.

God wants to use us, no matter our gifts or skills, to share the good news with the world. *What makes people special? People are special because we are made in God's image, as male and female, to know Him.*

LOW PREP

- construction paper
- envelopes
- crayons, markers, or colored pencils
- adhesive bandages
- googly eyes
- glue
- permanent marker

OPTION 2: Make get-well-soon cards

Provide supplies for kids to make get-well-soon cards. Suggest kids use the adhesive bandages like stickers. They can turn the bandages into people by gluing on googly eyes and adding arms, legs, and a smile with a permanent marker. Encourage them to write a message such as *Get well soon!* or *Praying for you!*

If someone from your class or church is ill or injured, consider making cards for that person. Otherwise, kids can leave the cards blank and give them to friends who get sick in the future. You may collect the cards to deliver to specific people or provide envelopes and allow kids to take the cards home for later use.

SAY • Being sick or hurt is no fun! When our bodies

don't work like they should, we might feel sad or frustrated. **People came to Jesus, and He healed them.** Jesus is the Son of God! One day, Jesus will take away all sickness and pain. When we trust in Him, we have forgiveness, salvation, and life with Him forever.

Option: Review the gospel with boys and girls. Explain that kids are welcome to speak with you or another teacher if they have questions.

Journal and prayer (5 minutes)

Distribute journal pages and pencils. Guide kids to think about and answer the questions listed on the page:

- What does this story teach me about God or the gospel?
- What does the story teach me about myself?
- Are there any commands in this story to obey? How are they for God's glory and my good?
- Are there any promises in this story to remember? How do they help me trust and love God?
- How does this story help me to live on mission better?

- pencils
- Journal Page
- "Scripture Survey" activity page, 1 per kid

As kids journal, invite them to share their ideas. Then pray, praising God for His power to perform miracles. Ask Him to meet kids' needs. Thank Him for sending His Son, Jesus, to meet their greatest need of all—to be rescued from sin and death.

As time allows, lead kids to complete "Scripture Survey" on the activity page. Kids should look up each Bible reference to answer the questions.

Tip: Give parents this week's *Big Picture Cards for Families* to allow families to interact with the biblical content at home.

Unit 21 · Session 2
Jesus Taught in Nazareth

BIBLE PASSAGE:
Luke 4

STORY POINT:
Jesus taught that He is the Messiah.

KEY PASSAGE:
John 3:16

BIG PICTURE QUESTION:
What makes people special? People are special because we are made in God's image, as male and female, to know Him.

INTRODUCE THE STORY (10–15 MINUTES) PAGE 182		TEACH THE STORY (25–30 MINUTES) PAGE 184		APPLY THE STORY (25–30 MINUTES) PAGE 190
	→		→	

Additional resources are available at gospelproject.com. For free training and session-by-session help, visit ministrygrid.com/gospelproject.

LEADER Bible Study

Jesus was about thirty years old when He began His earthly ministry. After John baptized Jesus in the Jordan River, Jesus was tempted in the desert. Jesus traveled to Jerusalem for the Passover. Then He headed north to Galilee. He went through the region of Samaria, stopping at Jacob's well to talk to a Samaritan woman.

After, Jesus went to the town of Nazareth, where He had grown up. Nazareth was a small village in the hills between the Sea of Galilee and the Mediterranean Sea. On the Sabbath day, Jesus went into the synagogue to teach. He read aloud the words of the prophet Isaiah. (See Isa. 61:1-2.) Jesus sat down. Everyone's eyes were on Him as He explained, "Today as you listen, this Scripture has been fulfilled." Jesus was saying, *It's Me*. The words Jesus read were coming true. Some people remembered Jesus from His youth. They asked, "Isn't this Joseph's son?"

Jesus knew their thoughts; Jesus had performed miracles in Capernaum, and the people wanted Jesus to do miracles in His hometown too. Jesus reminded them of two Old Testament accounts. Many widows lived in Israel when the prophet Elijah was there, but God sent Elijah to help a widow in another country. And Elisha likely encountered Israelites who had leprosy, but he healed Naaman the Syrian.

Jesus wanted the people to understand that His miracles were an act of grace—a gift. No one deserves God's grace, so God may show grace to whomever He pleases—even Gentiles. The people were angry about that last part. They drove Jesus away, intending to kill Him, but Jesus escaped through the crowd.

As you teach, explain that Jesus came to give sight to the blind and to set the captives free. He came preaching good news to all the people groups. Finally, the Messiah had come! Jesus was God's plan to save sinners.

The **BIBLE** Story

Jesus Taught in Nazareth
Luke 4

Jesus went to the town of Nazareth where He had lived when He was a boy. Now Jesus was grown. He traveled all around, teaching people about God. **On the Sabbath day, Jesus went to the synagogue in Nazareth.** The synagogue was a special building where Jews met together to pray, worship, and learn about the Scriptures.

Jesus stood up to read Scripture. He unrolled the scroll of the prophet Isaiah and read: "The Spirit of the Lord is on Me. He has chosen Me to tell good news to the poor. He has sent Me to tell the captives that they are free, to tell the blind that they can see, to free people who have been treated badly, and to announce that the Lord's favor is on us." Then Jesus rolled up the scroll. He gave it to the attendant and **sat down.**

Everyone in the synagogue stared at Jesus. **Jesus said, "Today as you listened to Me reading these words, they came true."**

The people said good things about Jesus, and they were amazed at Him. But some of the people in Nazareth had known Jesus from His youth. "Isn't this Joseph's son?" they asked. Jesus said, "No prophet is accepted in his hometown." Jesus told the people about times when God used prophets to help people who were not Jews. He reminded them of Elijah and Elisha. When there was a terrible famine in Israel and no rain fell there for three and a half years, plenty of widows in the country needed help. But **the prophet Elijah did not help the widows in Israel. Instead, God sent Elijah to help a widow in another land.**

And when Elisha was a prophet, many people in Israel had leprosy. They wanted to be healed, but Elisha did not heal them. Instead, he healed a man named Naaman (NAY muhn), and Naaman was from Syria—a country that hated God's people.

The people in the synagogue were angry. They forced Jesus out of town. They wanted to throw Him off a cliff, but Jesus walked right through the crowd and went on His way.

Christ Connection: Hundreds of years before Jesus was born, the prophet Isaiah wrote about God's plan to send a Messiah. The Messiah would bring good news and redeem people who were broken and hurting. Jesus read Isaiah's words and announced that He is the promised Messiah.

Bible Storytelling Tips

• **Stand and sit:** Begin the story seated. Stand when Jesus stands and sit back down when He sits.

• **Vary tone:** Speak boldly when speaking Jesus' words. Whisper the questions of the crowd.

INTRODUCE the Story

SESSION TITLE: Jesus Taught in Nazareth
BIBLE PASSAGE: Luke 4
STORY POINT: Jesus taught that He is the Messiah.
KEY PASSAGE: John 3:16
BIG PICTURE QUESTION: What makes people special? People are special because we are made in God's image, as male and female, to know Him.

Welcome time

Greet each kid as he or she arrives. Use this time to collect the offering, fill out attendance sheets, and help new kids connect to your group. Prompt kids to share about a favorite teacher they have had. What made that person a good teacher?

Activity page (5 minutes)

- "Who Is Jesus?" activity page, 1 per kid
- pencils or markers

Invite kids to complete "Who Is Jesus?" on the activity page. Guide kids to color in the spaces with two dots to discover who Jesus said He is.
SAY • What name did you discover in the spaces? (*Messiah*)
Do you remember what the name *Messiah* means? Explain that *Messiah* means "anointed one." In the Old Testament, prophets told about a Messiah who would come and rescue Israel. Jesus is the promised Messiah!

Session starter (10 minutes)

LOW PREP

- paper
- pencils

OPTION 1: Who is it?
Distribute paper and pencils. Tell kids to write their names at the bottom of their paper. Instruct each kid to write three to five sentences about herself. Consider giving prompts:

- Where were you born?
- How many people are in your family?
- What is your favorite color?
- What is your favorite thing to do?
- What do you want to be when you grow up?

Then collect the pages and read each one, allowing kids to guess who wrote the descriptions. After the group guesses, lead the kid who wrote the sentences to say, "It's me!"

SAY • In the Bible story we will hear today, Jesus read some words from the Scriptures. Then He said that the words were about Him!

OPTION 2: Accept it or reject it

Give each kid a red and green plate. Read a statement. If kids accept the statement as true, they should hold up the green plate. If they reject it as false, they should hold up the red one. Consider adding your own statements:

- red paper plates, 1 per kid
- green paper plates, 1 per kid

- A cat spent four years serving as the ceremonial mayor of a town in Minnesota. (*false; a dog*)
- A man in Germany once grew a pumpkin that weighed more than 2,500 pounds. (*true*)
- A bat eats 3 million insects each night. (*false; 3,000*)
- Eating too many carrots can turn your skin orange. (*true*)
- Your body's largest organ is your skin. (*true*)

SAY • When Jesus came to earth, He taught people the truth about God and His kingdom. Did everyone accept Jesus' words as true? No. Today we will hear about a time Jesus was rejected in His hometown.

Transition to teach the story

TEACH the Story

SESSION TITLE: Jesus Taught in Nazareth
BIBLE PASSAGE: Luke 4
STORY POINT: Jesus taught that He is the Messiah.
KEY PASSAGE: John 3:16
BIG PICTURE QUESTION: What makes people special? People are special because we are made in God's image, as male and female, to know Him.

Countdown

· countdown video

Show the countdown video as you transition to teach the story. Set it to end as the session begins.

Introduce the session (3 minutes)

· leader attire
· disposable gloves
· stethoscope
· clipboard
· Bible

Tip: If you prefer not to use themed content or characters, adapt or omit this introduction.

[Leader enters wearing dark pants, a solid-color shirt, disposable gloves, and a stethoscope. Leader carries a clipboard.]

LEADER • Hi there! I'm *[your name]*, a paramedic within the local emergency medical system. Every day, people experience injuries or illness and need care right away. My job requires assessing and providing initial treatment for patients in various places and transporting them to the hospital when necessary. When I'm not "on the field," you might find me at a library or in a classroom, educating the public about how to prevent injuries or illnesses and what they should do in an emergency. Making the public aware of ways they can help themselves in an emergency increases their chance of survival and allows first responders to focus on the most critical patients.

Some days, being a paramedic makes me imagine what Jesus must have encountered when He was on earth. He spent a lot of time healing people who were sick or injured, and He also spent a lot of time teaching people. Today, I want to tell you about something important Jesus taught about Himself.

Big picture question (1 minute)

LEADER • Does anyone remember our big picture question? Here it is: *What makes people special?* Does anyone have any ideas? [*Allow kids to respond.*] *People are special because we are made in God's image, as male and female, to know Him.* Now I'm going to ask the question again, and you say the answer together. *What makes people special? People are special because we are made in God's image, as male and female, to know Him.* Psalm 100:3 says that the Lord made us, and we are His. God tells us who He is through His Word, the Bible.

Giant timeline (1 minute)

Show the giant timeline. Point to individual Bible stories as you review.

·Giant Timeline

LEADER • The stories we've been learning about Jesus all happened early on in His ministry. Jesus came to earth and was born as a baby. **Jesus was born to be God's promised Savior.** We don't know a lot about Jesus when He was young but we know that **even as a child, Jesus wanted to do His Father's plan.**

Jesus was about 30 years old when His ministry began. **John the Baptist told people to follow Jesus.** Jesus began teaching people about God and His kingdom. In today's Bible story, Jesus taught in His hometown of Nazareth.

Among the People

Tell the Bible story (10 minutes)

- Bibles
- "Jesus Taught in Nazareth" video
- Big Picture Question Poster
- Bible Story Picture Poster
- Story Point Poster

Open your Bible to Luke 4. Use the Bible storytelling tips on the Bible story page to help you tell the story, or show the Bible story video "Jesus Taught in Nazareth."

LEADER • Nazareth was Jesus' hometown. Remember, Jesus was born in Bethlehem when Mary and Joseph traveled there to be counted for a census. When Jesus was still young, Mary and Joseph took Him to Nazareth, and Jesus grew up there. (Matt. 2:19-22)

Jesus went into the synagogue in Nazareth to teach on the Sabbath. He read from the scroll of the prophet Isaiah. What were the words that Jesus read from the scroll? Look at Luke 4:18-19. [*Allow kids to read the verse and respond.*]

When Jesus read these words, He said, "Today as you listen, this Scripture has been fulfilled." What did Jesus mean? Jesus was saying that those words Isaiah wrote were talking about Him! God chose Jesus to preach good news to the poor, to tell the captives that they are free, and to tell the blind that they can see. God promised throughout the Old Testament that a Messiah would come to rescue God's people. **Jesus taught that He is the Messiah!**

Jesus talked about the miracles some of the prophets, like Elijah and Elisha, did in the Old Testament. God had done good things for many people—not just the Jewish people. This made some of the people in the synagogue angry, and they rejected Jesus. They forced Him out of town and wanted to throw Jesus off a cliff, but Jesus walked away.

Christk connection

LEADER • Hundreds of years before Jesus was born, the prophet Isaiah wrote about God's plan to send a Messiah. The Messiah would bring good news and redeem people who were broken and hurting. Jesus read Isaiah's words and announced that He is the promised Messiah.

Though Jesus was rejected, His ministry continued. He came to earth to save people from their sins. Jesus never sinned, but He took the punishment we deserve when He died on the cross. Jesus was rejected at the cross so that everyone who trusts in Him will never be rejected by God. Everyone who trusts in Him is declared righteous and has eternal life.

Tip: Use Scripture and the guide provided on page 189 to explain how to become a Christian. Make sure kids know when and where they can ask questions.

Questions from kids video (3 minutes)

Show the "Unit 21, Session 2" questions from kids video. Prompt kids to think about why Jesus was rejected in Nazareth and why people might reject Jesus today. Guide them to discuss what they love about Jesus and what questions they have about following Him.

· "Unit 21, Session 2" questions from kids video

Missions moment (3 minutes)

Display the Las Vegas photos around the room or prepare to pass them around for kids to see. As they look, ask them to comment on some of the sites they see.

LEADER • Las Vegas, Nevada, is a busy city and a popular spot for tourists. Like many cities across the country, it's also a city where many people choose not to follow Jesus and are living without hope. Jesus taught that He is the Messiah, but many people still don't accept Him. Some Christians have chosen to live in

· "Las Vegas Photos" printable

Note: Kids will hear about specific missionaries in Nevada during session 3.

Among the People

Las Vegas as missionaries to teach people the truth about the gospel and the hope that Jesus gives. God wants all people to turn from sin and turn to Him. Pray, asking God to bring hope to the people of Las Vegas.

Key passage (5 minutes)

· Key Passage Poster
· "In This Way
  (John 3:16)" song

Show the key passage poster. Lead the boys and girls to read together John 3:16.

LEADER • God knew that sending His only Son to His enemies was going to be a costly mission. God loved the world, so He sent Jesus because His plan would use the death of His Son, Jesus, to rescue sinners. You see, the goal of God's plan is to take enemies and make them His friends forever. Let's sing.

Lead boys and girls in singing "In This Way (John 3:16)."

Sing (4 minutes)

· "Jesus Messiah" song
· Bible

Open your Bible and read aloud Psalm 96:1-3.

LEADER • **Jesus taught that He is the Messiah.** Jesus didn't come to bring salvation only to the Jews but to all people. *What makes people special? People are special because we are made in God's image, as male and female, to know Him.* Let's sing.

Sing together "Jesus Messiah."

Pray (2 minutes)

Invite kids to pray before dismissing to apply the story.

LEADER • Lord God, the gospel is good news! Thank You for Jesus—who releases the captives, gives sight to the blind, and frees the oppressed. We love You. Amen.

Dismiss to apply the story

The Gospel: God's Plan for Me

Ask kids if they have ever heard the word *gospel*. Clarify that the word *gospel* means "good news." It is the message about Christ, the kingdom of God, and salvation. Use the following guide to share the gospel with kids.

God rules. Explain to kids that the Bible tells us God created everything, and He is in charge of everything. Invite a volunteer to read Genesis 1:1 from the Bible. Read Revelation 4:11 or Colossians 1:16-17 aloud and explain what these verses mean.

We sinned. Tell kids that since the time of Adam and Eve, everyone has chosen to disobey God. (Romans 3:23) The Bible calls this sin. Because God is holy, God cannot be around sin. Sin separates us from God and deserves God's punishment of death. (Romans 6:23)

God provided. Choose a child to read John 3:16 aloud. Say that God sent His Son, Jesus, the perfect solution to our sin problem, to rescue us from the punishment we deserve. It's something we, as sinners, could never earn on our own. Jesus alone saves us. Read and explain Ephesians 2:8-9.

Jesus gives. Share with kids that Jesus lived a perfect life, died on the cross for our sins, and rose again. Because Jesus gave up His life for us, we can be welcomed into God's family for eternity. This is the best gift ever! Read Romans 5:8; 2 Corinthians 5:21; or 1 Peter 3:18.

We respond. Tell kids that they can respond to Jesus. Read Romans 10:9-10,13. Review these aspects of our response: Believe in your heart that Jesus alone saves you through what He's already done on the cross. Repent, turning from self and sin to Jesus. Tell God and others that your faith is in Jesus.

Offer to talk with any child who is interested in responding to Jesus. Provide *I'm a Christian Now!* for new Christians to take home and complete with their families.

APPLY the Story

SESSION TITLE: Jesus Taught in Nazareth
BIBLE PASSAGE: Luke 4
STORY POINT: Jesus taught that He is the Messiah.
KEY PASSAGE: John 3:16
BIG PICTURE QUESTION: What makes people special? People are special because we are made in God's image, as male and female, to know Him.

Key passage activity (5 minutes)

· Key Passage Poster

Option: Search online for motions using sign language.

Display the key passage poster. Lead kids in reading aloud John 3:16 together. Invite kids to choose motions for key words. You might suggesting the following:

- *God*—point upward
- *loved*—hug yourself
- *world*—form a circle with your arms
- *gave*—hold out hands, palms upward
- *one*—hold up one finger
- *everyone*—point to other people
- *eternal life*—stretch arms outward

Practice performing the motions as you say the key passage. Practice several times.

SAY • When He came to earth, **Jesus taught that He is the Messiah.** Jesus brings good news and redeems people who are broken and hurting. God loves us and wants us to know and love Him.

Discussion & Bible skills (10 minutes)

· Bibles, 1 per kid
· Story Point Poster
· Small Group Timeline and Map Set (005802970)

Distribute Bibles. Guide boys and girls to open their Bibles to Luke 4. Explain that more than half of the stories found in Luke are not found in Matthew; Mark; or John. Luke

Older Kids Leader Guide
Unit 21 • Session 2

was a doctor who wrote from eyewitness testimony to show that Jesus is both fully God and fully man, and He came to save all people—both Jews and Gentiles. Choose a volunteer to read Luke 4:21-22.

SAY • Jesus was in His hometown of Nazareth. [*Point to Nazareth (E5) on the New Testament Israel Map.*] Some of the people in the synagogue remembered Jesus from when He was a boy. They were surprised by Jesus' teaching. **Jesus taught that He is the Messiah.**

Ask the following questions. Lead the group to discuss:

Option: Retell or review the Bible story using the bolded text of the Bible story script.

1. What made Jesus different than other religious teachers? *Lead kids to recall that Jesus spoke with authority. He is the Word (John 1:1) and did not rely on tradition or other people to explain Scripture. Jesus came from heaven and is Lord over all things. He is God the Son and the promised Messiah.*
   (Option: Choose a volunteer to read Matt. 28:18.)

2. Jesus' promise to help everyone, no matter where they were from, upset the people in Nazareth. What does this tell you about God's heart and man's heart? *Help kids recognize that God loves all people. God's heart is full of mercy and love. Apart from Jesus, man's heart is full of envy, pride, and selfishness.*
   (Option: Choose a volunteer to read Phil. 2:3-4.)

3. Will Jesus always answer our prayers for healing? Why or why not? *Acknowledge that sin causes pain and suffering. Sometimes God chooses to answer our prayers for healing and restoration; other times He seems silent. We don't always understand God's plan, but He is good and one day He will make all things right.*
   (Option: Choose a volunteer to read Dan. 3:17-18.)

Activity choice (10 minutes)

 **OPTION 1:** Make a sign

Show the Las Vegas photos to kids. Point out the neon signs and colorful lights in the city.

SAY • Las Vegas is full of neon signs that mark popular tourist spots, restaurants, and hotels. Missionaries go into this busy city with all the neon lights to tell people about Jesus and start churches. **Jesus taught that He is the Messiah.** Let's make our own neon sign to let others know that we follow Jesus!

Distribute the supplies and direct kids to form the letters for *JESUS* with chenille stems and glue it to poster board or construction paper. Encourage them to hang their "neon sign" in their room or in a window. They might also ask their parents if they can display it in the car window this week. Encourage kids to share the love of Jesus every day.

OPTION 2: *Welcome* hunt

Write the letters *W-E-L-C-O-M-E* on separate sticky notes. Prior to small group, place the sticky notes on small, random objects throughout the room. Invite kids to hunt for letters.

Explain that there are seven letters scattered around the room. When a kid finds an object marked with a letter, he should bring that object to the center of the room.

After kids locate all seven letters, challenge them to work together to rearrange the letters to spell a word. (*welcome*)

Ask kids to share some ways they can make others feel welcome in their homes or at church.

SAY • Jesus was not welcome in His hometown of Nazareth, but He welcomes us into God's family. Jesus will never turn away anyone who comes to Him.

- "Las Vegas Photos" printable
- poster board (cut into smaller pieces) or construction paper
- colorful chenille stems (preferably in neon colors)
- glue

Tip: Use this activity option to reinforce the missions moment from Teach the Story.

 LOW PREP

- sticky notes
- marker

(John 6:37) Jesus gives eternal life to those who trust in Him, and believers will live with Him forever in heaven. We can welcome others into our homes, church, and classrooms. We can share with them the gospel—the good news about Jesus.

Hundreds of years before Jesus was born, the prophet Isaiah wrote about God's plan to send a Messiah. The Messiah would bring good news and redeem people who were broken and hurting. Jesus read Isaiah's words, and **Jesus taught that He is the promised Messiah.**

Option: Review the gospel with boys and girls. Explain that kids are welcome to speak with you or another teacher if they have questions.

Journal and prayer (5 minutes)

Distribute journal pages and pencils. Guide kids to think about and answer the questions listed on the page:

- What does this story teach me about God or the gospel?
- What does the story teach me about myself?
- Are there any commands in this story to obey? How are they for God's glory and my good?
- Are there any promises in this story to remember? How do they help me trust and love God?
- How does this story help me to live on mission better?

· pencils
· Journal Page
· "Trace the Travels" activity page, 1 per kid

As kids journal, invite them to share their ideas. Then pray, thanking Jesus for inviting everyone into God's family even though people rejected Jesus.

As time allows, lead kids to complete "Trace the Travels" on the activity page. Kids should look up each Bible reference to find where Jesus traveled. Then mark Jesus' journey on the map.

Tip: Give parents this week's *Big Picture Cards for Families* to allow families to interact with the biblical content at home.

Unit 21 · Session 3
Jesus and Nicodemus

BIBLE PASSAGE:
John 3

STORY POINT:
Jesus taught that we must be born again

KEY PASSAGE:
John 3:16

BIG PICTURE QUESTION:
What makes people special?
People are special because we are
made in God's image, as male and
female, to know Him.

INTRODUCE THE STORY (10–15 MINUTES) PAGE 198	TEACH THE STORY (25–30 MINUTES) PAGE 200	APPLY THE STORY (25–30 MINUTES) PAGE 206

 → →

Additional resources are available at gospelproject.com. For free training and session-by-session help, visit ministrygrid.com/gospelproject.

LEADER Bible Study

Jesus' ministry had begun. His early miracles included turning water into wine, casting out demons, and healing people. John 2:23 says that "many believed in his name when they saw the signs he was doing." Jesus likely spent a large part of His day teaching. When the day was done, He spent time alone or with His disciples. One night, a man named Nicodemus approached Jesus.

Nicodemus was a Pharisee and a ruler of the Jews; that is, he was a religious leader who taught God's law, and he was a member of the Sanhedrin—a Jewish governing body. Nicodemus held to the belief that if a person was a law-abiding Jew, he would be accepted by God. Jesus gave Nicodemus a lesson that would turn his belief system on its head.

Jesus was a carpenter (Mark 6:3), so the religious teachers likely assumed He didn't know theology. But they had seen Jesus' miraculous signs in Jerusalem. Nicodemus had to conclude, "You are a teacher who has come from God" (John 3:2).

Nicodemus initiated the conversation, but Jesus chose the subject. His words perplexed Nicodemus: "Unless someone is born again, he cannot see the kingdom of God" (John 3:3). Jesus explained that spiritual birth is not unlike physical birth in that a person cannot do it himself; it is something that happens to him.

Jesus reminded Nicodemus of an Old Testament account, the disobedient Israelites and the bronze snake. The Israelites could not help themselves, but when they trusted in God and looked to the bronze snake lifted up on the pole, they were healed. (Num. 21:4-9)

Emphasize to kids that every person is born a sinner—spiritually dead and alienated from God. It is by God's Spirit—not our own effort—that we are born again. We look to Jesus and His finished work on the cross for our salvation.

The **BIBLE** Story

Jesus and Nicodemus
John 3

Jesus was in Jerusalem for the Passover feast. **One night, a religious man came to see Jesus. The man's name was Nicodemus.** Nicodemus was a Pharisee. He studied and taught God's law, and he tried very hard to obey the law. **Nicodemus wanted to know more about Jesus.**

"Rabbi," he said, "we know that You are a teacher who has come from God. No one could do the miracles You do unless God were with him."

Nicodemus had that right. **Jesus said, "I tell you: Unless someone is born again, he cannot see the kingdom of God."**

Now Nicodemus was confused. He thought that keeping all God's laws was how a person got into heaven. Besides, what Jesus said didn't make any sense! **"How can anyone be born when he is old?"** **Nicodemus asked.**

Jesus said, **"A person cannot enter God's kingdom unless he is born of water and the Spirit.** Whatever is born of the flesh is flesh, and whatever is born of the Spirit is spirit." **When a baby is born, he gets physical life from his parents. Physical life doesn't last forever. But the Spirit gives people a better kind of life—spiritual life—so** they can live with God forever.

Jesus said, "Don't be surprised I told you that you must be born again."

Nicodemus still didn't understand. "How is this possible?" he asked.

Jesus said, "When you don't believe what I say about things I've seen on earth, how will you believe what I say about the things I've seen in heaven? **Do you remember how Moses raised up the bronze snake in the wilderness? Everyone who looked at it was healed. Like that, the Son of Man will be raised up, so that everyone who believes in Him will have eternal life.**"

Then Jesus told Nicodemus about God's great plan. Jesus said, "**God loved the world in this way: He gave His one and only Son, so that everyone who believes in Him will not perish but have eternal life.** God did not send His Son to declare the world guilty, but to save the world. Anyone who believes in Him is found not guilty, but anyone who does not believe in Him is guilty already."

Christ Connection: Nicodemus needed new life—eternal life—but he could not do anything to earn it. Eternal life is a gift that comes only from God. God showed His love in this way: He sent His one and only Son to save the world. Everyone who believes in Him will not perish but will have eternal life.

Bible Storytelling Tips

- **Call for active listening:** Challenge kids to count how many times they hear the word *born* in the story.
- **Vary your voice:** Vary your voice for the dialogue of different people. For example, use one voice for Jesus and another voice for Nicodemus.

INTRODUCE the Story

SESSION TITLE: Jesus and Nicodemus

BIBLE PASSAGE: John 3

STORY POINT: Jesus taught that we must be born again.

KEY PASSAGE: John 3:16

BIG PICTURE QUESTION: What makes people special? People are special because we are made in God's image, as male and female, to know Him.

Welcome time

Greet each kid as he or she arrives. Use this time to collect the offering, fill out attendance sheets, and help new kids connect to your group. Prompt kids to share who they go to when they have a question. Does that person always have the answers? Why?

Activity page (5 minutes)

- "Once or Twice" activity page, 1 per kid
- pencils or markers

Invite kids to complete "Once or Twice" on the activity page. Guide kids to use the key to decode the phrase that describes becoming God's child and receiving eternal life. (*born again*)

SAY • Your birthday is a celebration of the day you were born. Did you know if you trust in Jesus, you actually have *two* birthdays?! Today we are going to hear about Jesus' meeting with Nicodemus, and we will also learn what it means to be born again.

Session starter (10 minutes)

OPTION 1: Look-and-live tag

Play a game of freeze tag. Choose one player to be *It*. *It* will try to tag other players. If a player is tagged, she must freeze in place. She can only be unfrozen if another player stands in front of her and holds out his arms out to "heal" her and bring her back into the game. Play for a few minutes and then choose new players to be *It*.

SAY • Do you remember an Old Testament story about the Israelites' being bitten by snakes? God told them to look at a snake on a pole. When they did, they were healed. Jesus told a man about that story. We'll find out why.

OPTION 2: How in the world?

Write four questions on separate index cards regarding how things work. Examples of questions:

1. How can flies land on the ceiling?
2. How do glasses help people see?
3. Why is the ocean salty?
4. Why does ice cream cause a "brain freeze"?

Provide a pencil and two index cards to each kid. Read one question and invite kids to write a brief answer. Kids can write on the back and front of each index card.

If kids do not know the correct answer, encourage them to write their best guess. Then call for kids to read their answers. Let kids vote which answer they think is correct. Then give the correct explanation. Play again for each question.

SAY • Those were some hard questions to answer! Sometimes answers are difficult to understand! In the Bible story we will hear today, a man asked Jesus, "How can anyone be born when he is old?" We'll find out what Jesus said.

Transition to teach the story

· index cards, 2 per kid
· pencils

Answer Key:
1. Hairs on a fly's footpads produce sticky "glue" made of sugar and oil.
2. Eyeglasses bend light coming toward the eye to correct vision.
3. Rain breaks down rocks on land and washes salty elements (sodium and chloride) into the ocean.
4. The cold quickly constricts the blood vessels in the roof of your mouth.

TEACH the Story

SESSION TITLE: Jesus and Nicodemus
BIBLE PASSAGE: John 3
STORY POINT: Jesus taught that we must be born again.
KEY PASSAGE: John 3:16
BIG PICTURE QUESTION: What makes people special? People are special because we are made in God's image, as male and female, to know Him.

Countdown

· countdown video

Show the countdown video as you transition to teach the story. Set it to end as the session begins.

Introduce the session (3 minutes)

· leader attire
· disposable gloves
· stethoscope
· travel mug

Tip: If you prefer not to use themed content or characters, adapt or omit this introduction.

[Leader enters wearing dark pants, a solid-color shirt, and disposable gloves. Leader wears a stethoscope around his or her neck and carries a travel mug.]

LEADER • Hi there! It's me, [*your name*]. [*Sip from the travel mug.*] Whew, I am tired today. People need paramedics at all hours of the day, you know. I don't work a late shift very often, but I haven't quite caugh up on sleep from working a couple nights ago. Minc injuries, chest pain, and breathing problems are som of the common calls we receive. You never know what surprising call you're going to receive from dispatch. I want to share a Bible story with you toda about a time Jesus encountered a man at night. Let's find out what happened.

Big picture question (1 minute)

· Big Picture Question Poster

LEADER • Jesus met all kinds of people while He was on

earth, and He loved them. As you hear today's Bible story, think about our big picture question: *What makes people special? People are special because we are made in God's image, as male and female, to know Him.*

Say that with me: *What makes people special? People are special because we are made in God's image, as male and female, to know Him.*

God is not distant; He is personal and wants us to know Him. One way we can know better God is by reading His Word—the Bible.

Giant timeline (1 minute)

Show the giant timeline. Point to individual Bible stories as you review.

· Giant Timeline

LEADER • When Jesus traveled throughout the land of Judea, He changed the lives of many people He met. **People came to Jesus, and He healed them.** Jesus' miracles proved that Jesus is the Messiah, the Son of God. At the synagogue in Nazareth, Jesus read Isaiah's words and announced that He is the promised Messiah.

The people rejected Jesus, and He traveled to Jerusalem. That's where Jesus was when a man named Nicodemus came to talk to Him at night. Listen to this Bible story to find out what Jesus and Nicodemus talked to about.

· Bibles
· "Jesus and Nicodemus" video
· Big Picture Question Poster
· Bible Story Picture Poster
· Story Point Poster

Tell the Bible story (10 minutes)

Open your Bible to John 3. Use the Bible storytelling tips on the Bible story page to help you tell the story, or show the Bible story video "Jesus and Nicodemus."

Among the People

LEADER • After a long day of teaching, Jesus would spend His time alone or with His disciples. One night, when He was alone, a man came to visit Him. What was the man's name? (*Nicodemus*) Nicodemus was a Pharisee and a ruler of the Jews. That means he was a religious leader who taught God's law, and he was a leader in the Jewish government. Like other Jews, Nicodemus thought he knew how to be accepted by God—by obeying the laws. His encounter with Jesus changed him forever.

What did Jesus say must happen for a person to enter the kingdom of God? Look at John 3:5,7. [*Allow kids to read the verse and respond.*]

Jesus said, "Unless someone is born of water and the Spirit, he cannot enter the kingdom of God." When a baby is born, he gets physical life from his parents. Physical life doesn't last forever. But the Spirit gives people spiritual life so they can live with God forever.

Why did God send Jesus to earth? Look at John 3:16-17. [*Allow kids to read the verse and respond.*]

Christ connection

Tip: Use Scripture and the guide provided on page 205 to explain how to become a Christian. Make sure kids know when and where they can ask questions.

LEADER • Nicodemus needed new life—eternal life—but he could not do anything to earn it. Every person is born a sinner—spiritually dead and separated from God. Eternal life is a gift that comes only from God. It is by God's Spirit—not our own effort—that we are born again. We look to Jesus and His finished work on the cross for our salvation.

God showed His love in this way: He sent His

one and only Son to save the world. Everyone who believes in Him will not perish but will have eternal life.

Questions from kids video (3 minutes)

Show the "Unit 21, Session 3" questions from kids video. Prompt kids to think about what happens when a person trusts in Jesus. Guide them to discuss how they think a person might feel after trusting in Jesus. Would a person feel different? Why or why not?

· "Unit 21, Session 3" questions from kids video

 ## Missions moment (3 minutes)

LEADER • **Jesus taught that we must be born again.** As Christians, we want other people to know this, too. We can all have eternal life through Jesus. In Nevada, a young woman named Anna asked, "What can I do to have a relationship with Christ?" Missionaries Heiden and Neena Ratner and Christian athletes of Walk Church introduced Anna to Jesus and taught her how to be born again. Let's watch a video about her story.

· "Anna's Story" missions video

Play the "Anna's Story" missions video. Then pray that more people in Nevada will know Jesus and follow Him.

Key passage (5 minutes)

Show the key passage poster. Lead the boys and girls to read together John 3:16.

· Key Passage Poster
· "In This Way (John 3:16)" song

LEADER • There are lots of different people in the world, so who can get in on this good news? Anyone willing to come to God, to return to Him, to see Him for all that He is, and to receive His promise to save and rescue us from the wrath to come. This is happening

Among the People

all over the world. God is saving people from every tribe, tongue, people and nation. Let's sing.

Lead boys and girls in singing "In This Way (John 3:16)."

Sing (4 minutes)

· "Jesus Messiah" song
· Bible

Open your Bible and read aloud Psalm 96:10-11.

LEADER • Salvation is found in no other name than the name of Jesus. We are not saved by doing good works because our works would never be good enough. We are saved by putting our faith in Jesus, who lived the perfect life we failed to live and died the death we deserve for our sin. We rejoice in this good news. Let's sing.

Sing together "Jesus Messiah."

Pray (2 minutes)

Invite kids to pray before dismissing to apply the story.

LEADER • Lord God, we praise You because You are good. You saw us in our helplessness and loved us. You sent Your Son to bring light to the darkness and give life to the dead. Thank You for the gift of salvation through Jesus. You are all we need. Amen.

Dismiss to apply the story

The Gospel: God's Plan for Me

Ask kids if they have ever heard the word *gospel*. Clarify that the word *gospel* means "good news." It is the message about Christ, the kingdom of God, and salvation. Use the following guide to share the gospel with kids.

God rules. Explain to kids that the Bible tells us God created everything, and He is in charge of everything. Invite a volunteer to read Genesis 1:1 from the Bible. Read Revelation 4:11 or Colossians 1:16-17 aloud and explain what these verses mean.

We sinned. Tell kids that since the time of Adam and Eve, everyone has chosen to disobey God. (Romans 3:23) The Bible calls this sin. Because God is holy, God cannot be around sin. Sin separates us from God and deserves God's punishment of death. (Romans 6:23)

God provided. Choose a child to read John 3:16 aloud. Say that God sent His Son, Jesus, the perfect solution to our sin problem, to rescue us from the punishment we deserve. It's something we, as sinners, could never earn on our own. Jesus alone saves us. Read and explain Ephesians 2:8-9.

Jesus gives. Share with kids that Jesus lived a perfect life, died on the cross for our sins, and rose again. Because Jesus gave up His life for us, we can be welcomed into God's family for eternity. This is the best gift ever! Read Romans 5:8; 2 Corinthians 5:21; or 1 Peter 3:18.

We respond. Tell kids that they can respond to Jesus. Read Romans 10:9-10,13. Review these aspects of our response: Believe in your heart that Jesus alone saves you through what He's already done on the cross. Repent, turning from self and sin to Jesus. Tell God and others that your faith is in Jesus.

Offer to talk with any child who is interested in responding to Jesus. Provide *I'm a Christian Now!* for new Christians to take home and complete with their families.

APPLY the Story

SESSION TITLE: Jesus and Nicodemus

BIBLE PASSAGE: John 3

STORY POINT: Jesus taught that we must be born again.

KEY PASSAGE: John 3:16

BIG PICTURE QUESTION: What makes people special? People are special because we are made in God's image, as male and female, to know Him.

Key passage activity (5 minutes)

- Key Passage Poster
- paper
- pencils
- scissors (optional)

Display the key passage poster. Instruct kids to sit around a table and read John 3:16 aloud together. Give every kid a pencil and position a piece of paper in front of one kid.

Explain that when you say go, the first kid will write the first word of the key passage at the top of the paper and pass the paper to his left. The next kid will write the second word, pass the paper, and so on around the table until kids complete the verse.

Ask a kid to read the verse aloud to check their work. Then cut off or fold over the written verse and play again.

SAY • Our key passage comes from today's Bible story! To whom did Jesus say these words? (*Nicodemus*)

Invite volunteers to recite the key passage from memory.

Discussion & Bible skills (10 minutes)

- Bibles, 1 per kid
- Story Point Poster
- Small Group Timeline and Map Set (005802970)

Distribute Bibles. Guide boys and girls to open their Bibles to John 3. Explain that Nicodemus was a Pharisee, a ruler of the Jews. He came to Jesus at night in Jerusalem. [*Point out Jerusalem (H4) on the New Testament Israel Map.*]

SAY • **Jesus taught that we must be born again.** Without Jesus, we are spiritually dead. Our hearts are hard, and we love sin more than we love God. But God can soften people's hearts. Jesus offers new life to those who trust in Him for salvation. Let's answer our big picture question: **What makes people special? People are special because we are made in God's image, as male and female, to know Him.**

Choose a volunteer to read aloud John 3:14-16. Ask the following questions. Lead the group to discuss:

Option: Retell or review the Bible story using the bolded text of the Bible story script.

1. How was the bronze serpent being lifted up like Jesus being lift up? *Lead kids to connect that like the serpent, Jesus was lifted up on the cross. He died for our sins and was raised from the dead. Like the Israelites with snakebites, we can't do anything to save ourselves. But we can look to Jesus for salvation.*
(Option: Choose a volunteer to read Num. 21:8-9.)

2. Can a person get into heaven by doing enough good things? Why or why not? *Emphasize that God wants us to obey Him, but the Bible says everyone sins. (Rom. 3:23) If we had to obey God perfectly to go to heaven, no one would ever get to heaven! We are accepted by God when we trust in Jesus, who lived a perfect life and died the death we deserve for our sins.*
(Option: Choose a volunteer to read Eph. 2:8-9.)

3. How is being apart from God like being in the dark? How can we bring friends and family members into the light of the gospel? *Explain to kids that the Bible says that Jesus is the light of the world. Before we trust in Jesus, we live in darkness. Discuss the difficulty of seeing in the dark. God lights up the path of our lives and shows us what is true. We can tell others about what Jesus has done and pray for them.*
(Option: Choose a volunteer to read Eph. 5:8-10.)

Tip: Use this activity option to reinforce the missions moment from Teach the Story.

Activity choice (10 minutes)

OPTION 1: Prepare the way

Write the following phrases on construction paper and put the papers on the floor around your room:

1. *Make Friends*
2. *Eat a Meal Together*
3. *Explore the City*
4. *Invite them to Your Home*
5. *Give them a Bible*
6. *Talk about Jesus*
7. *Pray for Your Friend*
8. *Invite them to Church*
9. *Enjoy Spending Time with Them*
10. *Tell Them How to Become a Christian*

Make a simple path around the room with the papers. Prepare to take your kids on a "journey with missionaries" who are preparing the way for people to come to Jesus.

SAY • Missionaries like Heiden and Neena Ratner in Las Vegas, Nevada, are leading people to Jesus. Let's take a walk around the room and see some of the things a missionary does to lead people to Jesus. We can do these things, too!

Walk the path together, stopping at each paper and asking a volunteer to read the words. Ask kids to share examples of how they might tell someone about Jesus, using these steps.

· Allergy Alert
· disposable bowl
· 1 cup of water
· 1½ cups cornstarch
· paper towels or wet wipes (for cleanup)
· spoon (optional)

OPTION 2: Make *oobleck*

Demonstrate how to make *oobleck*, a substance that acts like both a solid and a liquid. First, pour 1 cup of water into a disposable bowl. Gradually add 1½ cups cornstarch. Stir thoroughly or mix with your hands. Adjust the consistency of the oobleck by adding more water or cornstarch.

Show kids how the oobleck reacts to touch by slowly pulling your fingers through it. It will flow and drip like a liquid. Poke or punch the oobleck. Applying pressure to the mixture will make it will feel hard like a solid.

If you wish, allow kids to experiment with the oobleck. Invite them to knead it, roll it, or pour it. Provide paper towels or wet wipes for cleanup.

Remind kids that **Jesus taught that we must be born again** to enter God's kingdom.

SAY • Without Jesus, we are spiritually dead. Our hearts are hard, and we love sin more than we love God. But God can soften people's hearts. Jesus offers new life to those who trust in Him for salvation.

Option: Review the gospel with boys and girls. Explain that kids are welcome to speak with you or another teacher if they have questions.

Journal and prayer (5 minutes)

Distribute journal pages and pencils. Guide kids to think about and answer the questions listed on the page:

- What does this story teach me about God or the gospel?
- What does the story teach me about myself?
- Are there any commands in this story to obey? How are they for God's glory and my good?
- Are there any promises in this story to remember? How do they help me trust and love God?
- How does this story help me to live on mission better?

· pencils
· Journal Page
· "Crossing Paths" activity page, 1 per kid

As kids journal, invite them to share their ideas. Then pray, thanking God for making the way for us to have new life when we trust in Jesus.

As time allows, lead kids to complete "Crossing Paths" on the activity page. Kids should use the clues and Bible references to complete the crossword puzzle.

Tip: Give parents this week's *Big Picture Cards for Families* to allow families to interact with the biblical content at home.

Among the People

Unit 21 • Session 4
Jesus and the Samaritan Woman

BIBLE PASSAGE:
John 4

STORY POINT:
Jesus gives the Holy Spirit
to those who believe.

KEY PASSAGE:
John 3:16

BIG PICTURE QUESTION:
What makes people special?
People are special because we are
made in God's image, as male and
female, to know Him.

INTRODUCE THE STORY	TEACH THE STORY	APPLY THE STORY
(10–15 MINUTES)	(25–30 MINUTES)	(25–30 MINUTES)
PAGE 214	PAGE 216	PAGE 222

 → →

Additional resources are available at gospelproject.com. For free training and session-by-session help, visit ministrygrid.com/gospelproject.

LEADER Bible Study

At the time Jesus was on earth, Jews and Samaritans didn't get along. The strife between the two groups stretched back hundreds of years, to the Babylonian exile.

When the Babylonians attacked Judah, they moved a large group of God's people away from their homes. But some of the people—the poorest, sickest, least able to work—were left behind in the region that became known as Samaria. The exile lasted 70 years. During that time, those left in Samaria began to mingle with their neighbors to the north. They intermarried and practiced foreign customs. While the Samaritans still believed in God, they adapted foreign beliefs as well.

The Jews who returned home from Babylon to rebuild God's temple in Jerusalem rejected this new way of life. They were dedicated to obeying and worshiping God, so they didn't agree with the Samaritans' practices. The Samaritans opposed the Jews' efforts to reestablish their nation. In time, the Jews' hate for the Samaritans grew—so much so that a Jew traveling from Judea to Galilee would take a longer route to travel around Samaria rather than through it.

Jesus broke down barriers when He traveled to Galilee by way of Samaria. Even more surprising, Jesus stopped at a well around noon and asked a Samaritan woman for a drink. Jewish men did not speak to women in public.

But Jesus was kind to her, and He offered her a gift: living water. The woman didn't understand, but Jesus revealed His knowledge of her past. He even gave her a glimpse of the future. The Samaritan woman expected a Messiah to come and fix everything. Jesus said, "I am He."

Explain to kids that the living water Jesus offers is the Holy Spirit. (See John 7:37-39.) The Holy Spirit is a gift that He is eager to give us when we ask Him. Those who receive His grace will never be thirsty again.

Among the People

The **BIBLE** Story

Jesus and the Samaritan Woman
John 4

Jesus had been teaching in Judea. He **and His disciples** began traveling back to Galilee. They **traveled through Samaria and stopped in a town with a well. Jesus' disciples went into town to buy food. While Jesus was at the well, a Samaritan woman came to get water from the well. Jesus said to her, "Give Me a drink."**

The woman was surprised. **"Why are You talking to me?"** she asked. **"You're a Jew, and I'm a Samaritan."**

Jesus said, **"I asked you for a drink. You don't know who I am. If you did, you would have asked Me for a drink, and I would give you living water."**

The woman was confused. She **said,** "Sir, this well is deep, and You don't have a bucket. **Where do You get this 'living water'?"**

Jesus said, **"Anyone who drinks this well water will be thirsty again, but whoever drinks from the water I give will never be thirsty again! In fact, the water I give will become a well inside you, and you will have eternal life."** Jesus was talking about the Holy Spirit, but the woman did not understand.

"Sir," she said, **"give me this water. If I'm not thirsty, I won't have**

to keep coming to this well to get water."

"Go get your husband," Jesus said.

"I don't have a husband," the woman replied.

Jesus knew she was telling the truth. He said, "You don't have a husband now, but you've had five husbands."

Jesus was right. "I see You are a prophet," the woman said. Maybe this prophet could explain something to her. She said, "The Samaritans worship here on a mountain, but the Jews say we need to worship at the temple in Jerusalem."

Jesus said, "Soon you will not need to be in either of those places to worship God in spirit and in truth."

The woman said, "I know the Messiah is coming. When He comes, He will explain everything to us."

Then Jesus said, "I am the Messiah."

The woman left and told the people in her town, "Come, see a man who told me everything I ever did! Could this be the Messiah?"

Many Samaritans believed in Jesus because of what the woman said. Jesus stayed in their town for two days. **Many more believed because of what Jesus said. They told the woman, "We no longer believe because of what you said, for we have heard for ourselves and know that this really is the Savior of the world."**

Christ Connection: Jesus offers something better than physical water; He gives us Himself. Jesus gives the Holy Spirit to everyone who comes to Him by faith. We can worship Him as Lord and Savior wherever we are.

Bible Storytelling Tips

- **Use props:** Carry a bucket or water jug as you tell the Bible story.
- **Display a map:** Show a Bible times map and point out the locations of Judea, Galilee, and Samaria. Consider using the New Testament Israel Map from the Small Group Timeline and Map Set (005802970).

Among the People

INTRODUCE the Story

SESSION TITLE: Jesus and the Samaritan Woman

BIBLE PASSAGE: John 4

STORY POINT: Jesus gives the Holy Spirit to those who believe.

KEY PASSAGE: John 3:16

BIG PICTURE QUESTION: What makes people special? People are special because we are made in God's image, as male and female, to know Him.

Welcome time

Greet each kid as he or she arrives. Use this time to collect the offering, fill out attendance sheets, and help new kids connect to your group. Prompt kids to share about their favorite drinks. Which drinks are best when you're really thirsty?

Activity page (5 minutes)

· "Big Picture Jars" activity page, 1 per kid
· pencils or markers

Invite kids to complete "Big Picture Jars" on the activity page. Guide kids to use the pictures in the jars to fill in the answer to the big picture question.

SAY • Do you believe that all people are special? The Bible says they are! In the Bible story we are going to hear today, Jesus traveled through a place called Samaria and met a woman who some people did not think was very special or important. Do you think Jesus talked to her? Why? Let's find out more.

LOW PREP

· paper
· pencils

Session starter (10 minutes)

OPTION 1: Partner poll

Give each kid a piece of paper and a pencil. Form pairs of kids. Instruct kids to number their papers from 1 to 10.

Older Kids Leader Guide
Unit 21 • Session 4

Explain that you will give 10 prompts, and kids should write down the answers they think best apply to their partner. Then read the prompts again and allow partners to share their answers with each other. Invite volunteers to share what they wrote and let the partner reveal if the answer is correct or not.

Suggested Prompts:
1. favorite color
2. family size
3. birthday
4. birth place
5. favorite food
6. favorite season
7. favorite song
8. height
9. number of pets
10. favorite school subject

SAY • How well do you know other people? In today's Bible story, Jesus met a woman who had never met Him before. He knew everything about her!

OPTION 2: Reversing arrow demonstration
Draw two parallel left-facing arrows on white heavyweight paper. Position the paper behind a glass cup so kids can see the arrows through the glass.

· white heavyweight paper
· black marker
· glass cup
· water

Slowly pour water into the glass until the water level is just above the bottom arrow. The arrow should flip horizontally, appearing as a right-facing arrow.

Move the cup to show kids that the drawn arrows still face to the left. Return the cup to its place in front of the arrows. Add more water so the top arrow appears to change directions as well.

Tip: Practice this demonstration before the session to determine the correct distance required between the cup and arrows to achieve the illusion.

SAY • How did that happen? [*Invite kids to explain.*] Nothing is special about this water; this demonstration is an example of *refraction*—light bending when it passes through different materials (like air, glass, and water). In the story we will hear today, Jesus told a woman He could give her living water. It wasn't a trick, though. Let's find out what Jesus was talking about.

Transition to teach the story

TEACH the Story

SESSION TITLE: Jesus and the Samaritan Woman
BIBLE PASSAGE: John 4
STORY POINT: Jesus gives the Holy Spirit to those who believe.
KEY PASSAGE: John 3:16
BIG PICTURE QUESTION: What makes people special? People are special because we are made in God's image, as male and female, to know Him.

Countdown

· countdown video

Show the countdown video as you transition to teach the story. Set it to end as the session begins.

Introduce the session (3 minutes)

· leader attire
· disposable gloves
· stethoscope
· first aid kit
· Bible

Tip: If you prefer not to use themed content or characters, adapt or omit this introduction.

[Leader enters wearing dark pants, a solid-color shirt, and disposable gloves. Leader wears a stethoscope around his or her neck and carries a first aid kit.]

LEADER • Hi there! It's me, *[your name]*. Did you know that paramedics don't always travel in ambulances? Sometimes we set up a tent and work an event—like a concert or soccer game. When a large crowd gathers, especially when it's hot outside, there is a good chance someone will end up needing medical attention. We can treat everything from minor scrapes to sunburns and dehydration. As medical professionals, we never refuse treatment to anyone. Even if the person was injured because he made a poor decision, every life is important.

I want to share a Bible story with you today about a time Jesus encountered someone who was surprised that Jesus paid any attention to her.

Big picture question (1 minute)

LEADER • Our big picture question fits right into our Bible story. I'll ask the question, and then I want you to shout out the answer: *What makes people special? People are special because we are made in God's image, as male and female, to know Him.* Isn't that great? God wants all people—no matter where they are from, what they look like, or what activities they like—to know Him. He created each of us in His image and He gave us His Word, the Bible, so we can know what is true about God and about ourselves.

· Big Picture Question Poster

Giant timeline (1 minute)

Show the giant timeline. Point to individual Bible stories as you review.

· Giant Timeline

LEADER • Jesus spent a lot of time with people while He was on earth. He is *Immanuel*—"God with us"! Who are some of the people we've heard about the last few weeks? [*Invite kids to respond.*] We saw that **people came to Jesus, and He healed them.** He met with people in the synagogue, and **Jesus taught that He is the Messiah.**

Did everyone believe Him? Not exactly. Many people didn't understand. Nicodemus went to talk to Jesus at night. **Jesus taught that we must be born again.** In today's story, "Jesus and the Samaritan Woman," we will see how Jesus interacted with all people—not just Jews.

Tell the Bible story (10 minutes)

Open your Bible to John 4. Use the Bible storytelling tips on the Bible story page to help you tell the story, or show

· Bibles
· "Jesus and the Samaritan Woman" video
· Big Picture Question Poster
· Bible Story Picture Poster
· Story Point Poster

the Bible story video "Jesus and the Samaritan Woman."

LEADER • Jesus and His disciples were traveling from Judea to Galilee. The fastest way home was to go through Samaria. Most Jews took the long way around because Jews and Samaritans didn't get along. But Jesus went through Samaria and stopped at a well there. Whom did Jesus meet at the well? (*a Samaritan woman*) She was surprised that a Jewish man would talk to her. Jesus offered the woman living water. **Jesus gives the Holy Spirit to those who believe.**

What did the woman learn about Jesus? Look at John 4:19. [*Allow kids to read the verse and respond.*] The woman believed He was a prophet. She was right, but that's not all Jesus is. What else did the woman learn about Jesus? Look at John 4:25-26. [*Allow kids to read the verse and respond.*] Jesus revealed that He is the Messiah she was waiting for. The woman told other people from her town about Jesus, and Jesus stayed with them for two days. What did they learn about who Jesus is? Look at John 4:42. [*Allow kids to read the verse and respond.*]

Christ connection

LEADER • Jesus offers something better than physical water; He gives us Himself. Jesus gives the Holy Spirit to everyone who comes to Him by faith. He completely satisfies us. He is the Prophet who gives us power to worship Him as Lord and Savior wherever we are. Jesus is the Messiah who brings salvation for all who trust in Him.

Tip: Use Scripture and the guide provided on page 221 to explain how to become a Christian. Make sure kids know when and where they can ask questions.

Questions from kids video (3 minutes)

Show the "Unit 21, Session 4" questions from kids video. Prompt kids to think about how Jesus showed love to people while He was on earth. Guide them to discuss how we can show love to others, especially those who might seem hard to love.

· "Unit 21, Session 4" questions from kids video

LEADER • *What makes people special? People are special because we are made in God's image, as male and female, to know Him.*

Missions moment (3 minutes)

Display the "Walk Church in Prayer" printable and ask a volunteer to read the caption. Stop and pray, or ask for a volunteer to pray according to the provided prompt.

· "Walk Church in Prayer" printable

LEADER • The Ratners and the Christians at Walk Church believe in the power of prayer and that the Holy Spirit will help them share Jesus with more people. **Jesus gives the Holy Spirit to those who believe.** Let's pray that the Holy Spirit will help the Ratners and missionaries all over the world.

Key passage (5 minutes)

Show the key passage poster. Lead the boys and girls to read together John 3:16.

· Key Passage Poster
· "In This Way (John 3:16)" song

LEADER • Everyone is in danger of perishing, or dying and being separated from God forever. The Bible tells us a day is coming when everyone will have to pay for sin. Jesus is saying here that He is willing to pay for our sins. We just need to trust Him, follow Him, and believe that He is able to save us from the wrath of God that is coming on the world that God loves. This rescue is by faith. Now we are waiting for Jesus to return and when He does, life with Him will begin and never end. That's good news! Let's sing. Lead boys and girls in singing "In This Way (John 3:16)."

Sing (4 minutes)

· "Take It to the Lord"
song
· Bible

Open your Bible and read aloud Psalm 99:4-5.

LEADER • Jesus is worthy. He is just, righteous, and holy. He knows our every weakness and loves us. We can worship the Lord wherever we are. Let's sing to Him.

Sing together "Take It to the Lord."

Pray (2 minutes)

Invite kids to pray before dismissing to apply the story.

LEADER • Lord God, apart from You we are thirsty! You provide living water—Your Spirit—through Jesus. Forgive us for seeking satisfaction in things like popularity, other people, or personal comfort. We need You. Give us boldness to share the good news of the gospel with others. We love You. Amen.

Dismiss to apply the story

The Gospel: God's Plan for Me

Ask kids if they have ever heard the word *gospel*. Clarify that the word *gospel* means "good news." It is the message about Christ, the kingdom of God, and salvation. Use the following guide to share the gospel with kids.

God rules. Explain to kids that the Bible tells us God created everything, and He is in charge of everything. Invite a volunteer to read Genesis 1:1 from the Bible. Read Revelation 4:11 or Colossians 1:16-17 aloud and explain what these verses mean.

We sinned. Tell kids that since the time of Adam and Eve, everyone has chosen to disobey God. (Romans 3:23) The Bible calls this sin. Because God is holy, God cannot be around sin. Sin separates us from God and deserves God's punishment of death. (Romans 6:23)

God provided. Choose a child to read John 3:16 aloud. Say that God sent His Son, Jesus, the perfect solution to our sin problem, to rescue us from the punishment we deserve. It's something we, as sinners, could never earn on our own. Jesus alone saves us. Read and explain Ephesians 2:8-9.

Jesus gives. Share with kids that Jesus lived a perfect life, died on the cross for our sins, and rose again. Because Jesus gave up His life for us, we can be welcomed into God's family for eternity. This is the best gift ever! Read Romans 5:8; 2 Corinthians 5:21; or 1 Peter 3:18.

We respond. Tell kids that they can respond to Jesus. Read Romans 10:9-10,13. Review these aspects of our response: Believe in your heart that Jesus alone saves you through what He's already done on the cross. Repent, turning from self and sin to Jesus. Tell God and others that your faith is in Jesus.

Offer to talk with any child who is interested in responding to Jesus. Provide *I'm a Christian Now!* for new Christians to take home and complete with their families.

APPLY the Story

SESSION TITLE: Jesus and the Samaritan Woman

BIBLE PASSAGE: John 4

STORY POINT: Jesus gives the Holy Spirit to those who believe.

KEY PASSAGE: John 3:16

BIG PICTURE QUESTION: What makes people special? People are special because we are made in God's image, as male and female, to know Him.

Key passage activity (5 minutes)

- Key Passage Poster
- foam or plastic cups, 30
- permanent marker

Tip: The CSB® translation fits two words per cup with the last word and reference on the fifteenth cup.

Before the session, write the key passage and words and phrases on 15 cups. Make two sets. Mix up the order of each set. Display the key passage poster. Lead kids in reading aloud John 3:16 together.

Form two teams. Give each team a set of cups and challenge them to build a pyramid, arranging the cups in order with the first word of the key passage on the top row. This may require some planning.

SAY • How did God show His love for us? He sent His Son to rescue us!

Discussion & Bible skills (10 minutes)

- Bibles, 1 per kid
- Story Point Poster
- Small Group Timeline and Map Set (005802970)

Distribute Bibles. Guide boys and girls to open their Bibles to John 4. Explain that Jesus traveled through the land of Samaria on His way to Galilee from Judea. [*Display the New Testament Israel Map and point out the land of Judea (J3), the land of Samaria (F4), and the land of Galilee (C5).*]

SAY • **Jesus gives the Holy Spirit to those who believe.** Choose a volunteer to read aloud John 4:13-14. Ask the following questions. Lead the group to discuss:

1. What is living water? Where does it comes from?

Guide kids to recall that Jesus offered living water to the
Samaritan woman. The living water Jesus was talking
about is the Holy Spirit. Jesus gives the Holy Spirit to
those who trust in Him. He saves us from our sins and
gives us eternal life.

Option: Retell or review the Bible story using the bolded text of the Bible story script.

(Option: Choose a volunteer to read John 7:37-39.)

2. Why is sharing your testimony important? *Help*
   kids recognize the power of the Samaritan woman's
   testimony. She told others in her town what Jesus had
   done, and they believed in Him. Emphasize that
   everyone can tell others what God has done in his or her
   life. Jesus calls us to build relationships with others and
   tell them the good news of the gospel.

   (Option: Choose a kid to read 1 John 4:13-15.)

3. What are some ways you can show love to others?
   How can you remember to put others first? *Allow*
   kids to share their ideas for practically serving others.
   Suggest kids paint one fingernail a bright color, wear
   their watch upside-down, apply a sticker to a place
   they'll see frequently (such as the toe of a shoe). When
   kids see the paint, watch, or sticker, they can remember
   to live with an others-first attitude.

   (Option: Choose a volunteer to read 1 John 4:11.)

Activity choice (10 minutes)

OPTION 1: Picture prayers

Display a map of the United States. Distribute
sticky notes and crayons. Invite kids to think of ways
they can pray for Christians at Walk Church and other
Christians who are sharing the gospel in Nevada.

· map of the United States
· yarn
· sticky notes
· crayons
· tape

Ask kids to write their prayer request on the sticky note
or draw a picture representing that request. For example,

Tip: Use this activity option to reinforce the missions moment from Teach the Story.

Option: Display the map for a few weeks to remind kids to pray for missionaries.

a kid might draw a Bible to represent prayers that more people will learn about the Bible.

Allow each kid to tape a piece of yarn from your state to Nevada. Then add the sticky note. Take time to pray for missionaries, asking volunteers to pray aloud.

SAY • Praying is a very important and powerful way that we support missionaries and churches around the world. That's why people ask us to please pray for them. They know that our prayers matter!

· bottled waters
· Bibles

OPTION 2: Bottle flip review game

Form two teams of kids. Invite players to take turns flipping a bottle of water, trying to land it upside down on its lid or upright on its bottom. When a player lands a flip, ask her team a review question. Correct answers earn 5 points for an upright bottle and 10 points for an upside-down bottle.

1. Where were Jesus and His disciples headed? (*Galilee, John 4:3*)
2. In what land did Jesus and His disciples stop at a well? (*Samaria, John 4:4-6*)
3. Who came to the well when Jesus was there? (*a Samaritan woman, John 4:7*)
4. What did Jesus first say to the woman? (*"Give me a drink," John 4:7*)
5. Why was the woman surprised that Jesus was talking to her? (*Jews did not associate with Samaritans, John 4:9*)
6. What did Jesus say He could give the woman? (*living water, John 4:10*)
7. What kind of life did Jesus say living water brings? (*eternal life, John 4:14*)
8. Who did the woman think Jesus was? (*a prophet,*